TRICKS THAT
TAKE FISH

TRICKS THAT
TAKE FISH

THE DEFINITIVE GUIDE TO CATCHING FRESHWATER GAMEFISH ON BAIT, LURES, AND FLIES

HAROLD BLAISDELL
FOREWORD BY H. G. TAPPLY
INTRODUCTION BY JAY CASSELL

Skyhorse Publishing

Skyhorse Publishing books may be purchased in bulk at special discounts for sales promotion, corporate gifts, fund-raising, or educational purposes. Special editions can also be created to specifications. For details, contact the Special Sales Department, Skyhorse Publishing, 307 West 36th Street, 11th Floor, New York, NY 10018 or info@skyhorsepublishing.com.

Skyhorse® and Skyhorse Publishing® are registered trademarks of Skyhorse Publishing, Inc.®, a Delaware corporation.

www.skyhorsepublishing.com

10 9 8 7 6 5 4 3 2 1

Library of Congress Cataloging-in-Publication Data is available on file.
ISBN: 978-1-61608-695-4

Illustrations by Walter Dower

Printed in the United States of America

Contents

FOREWORD... *vii*
INTRODUCTION..*ix*

I. **TAKING TROUT
     ON BAIT** I

2. **FLY FISHING**...........................36

3. **SPINNING** 74

4. **BAIT FISHING
     FOR BASS**...........................90

5. **PLUGS, BUGS,
     AND HARDWARE** 117

6. LAKE TROUT AND SALMON 148

7. PICKEREL, PIKE, AND MUSKELLUNGE 167

8. PANFISH 189

9. ICE FISHING 205

10. A FEW ODDS AND ENDS 225

Foreword

Several years ago I started a collection of tricks that had helped me to take fish when orthodox methods failed. The collection took the form of scribbled memos like "Rubber strip on tail hook of bass plug" and "Live nymph on No.-14 hook, good low water." These I tucked away in a large Manila envelope, my intent at the time being to gather such pearls of angling wisdom until I had enough for a magazine article. This I planned to title "Tricks That Take Fish" and to sell for cash.

But alas, my collection grew slowly, and I had all but abandoned it when, three trout seasons ago, I started fishing with Harold Blaisdell. Immediately the Manila envelope began to fatten at a prodigious rate with newly discovered tricks that took fish. Soon I had enough for a major magazine feature. Before I could write it I had enough for two. As I scribbled notes after an especially rewarding day on the Battenkill with Blaisdell, I dared think I might soon have enough tricks for a book.

So one day I began sorting them out. At first I felt greatly cheered to find I had scores of proven, practical fish-taking tricks that fishermen everywhere could use with profit on almost every game fish that inhabits fresh water. Then, as I continued my inventory, my cheer turned to dismay. Of all these fish-taking tricks, barely half a dozen were mine. The rest were Blaisdell's. Night fishing for big trout with a skinned minnow, that was his. Fishing with whips for winter walleyes, that was his, too. The notes betrayed my perfidy, and in my own handwriting, too. I still didn't have enough tricks of my own to get beyond six paragraphs of a magazine article.

It so happens that Harold Blaisdell is as capable of writing a book as I, and quite probably more so. His stories of fishing and gunning have delighted the readers of all the country's leading outdoor magazines. He writes with the same grace and skill with which he handles a fishing rod. Were this not so, I should have written this book myself and given him credit in the Foreword for the many ideas which he contributed to my literary effort.

But since Harold possesses both the time and talent for book-writing and since the ideas herein contained are his except for my meager half-dozen, I feel it only fair to divide the project thusly: Harold to write the book and I the Foreword.

Just remember, though, that sticking a strip of rubber on the tail hook of a bass plug was *my* idea.

—H. G. Tapply

Introduction

A number of years ago, I picked up a book at a sporting-goods store near my home. Titled *The Art of Fishing with Worms and Other Live Bait*, the book's subtitle promised that this was "A modern guide to the oldest form of fishing—a first resort for some anglers, a last resort for others, but seldom practiced by anyone with the skills revealed by Harold F. Blaisdell."

A book primarily on worm fishing? You're kidding, I thought to myself. Everybody knows how to fish with worms, don't they? The more I thought about it, though, and as I thumbed through the book's pages, the more I realized that there are subtleties to worm and bait fishing, just as there are subtleties to fly fishing, spin fishing, and bait casting (with plugs). I bought the book—hey, maybe I'd learn something. And if I didn't, I didn't.

I did—big time. As I read through that book, I learned more about worm fishing than I thought was possible. How to properly impale a nightcrawler onto a hook, how to weight the bait properly, how to cast in stream or lake, where to cast, how to deal with clear water, or turbid water. It was all there—and I have to say, coming away from that book, I knew I was a better angler, because the author taught me to look at things differently, to think like a trout (or bass, or panfish), to analyze everything before even wetting a line. What I especially liked about that book was Blaisdell's easy-to-read, no-nonsense style.

So, now along comes *The Pocket Guide to Tricks That Take Fish*. This isn't just on bait fishing, though. This is on everything—fly, spinning, bait, plugs, hardware, even ice fishing tackle. Written in Blaisdell's straightforward, analytical style, the book takes you through all of the major freshwater gamefish. Want to catch trout in a stream? Blaisdell will tell you how, in a no-nonsense manner, with fly, lure, or bait. Smallmouth or largemouth on bait? No problem—the author will tell you where to look in a given water, what to use, how to rig up, how to cast, and how to fight a hooked fish. Lake trout? Panfish? Pike-pickerel-muskie? They're all here, along with others.

Whether you're new to the sport of fishing, or a veteran angler with years under your belt, you're going to learn something by reading this tip book. And that means you're going to catch more fish. And that's what it's all about.

—Jay Cassell

1. Taking Trout on Bait

WHENEVER A FELLOW FISHERMAN TELLS ME CURTLY that he never uses natural bait for game fish because it "takes no skill to catch fish on bait," I merely force a grin and change the subject.

Just because the veriest dub can catch an occasional fish on bait doesn't mean that he can't do the same with a fly or other artificial lure. It doesn't mean, either, that it is any easier to become an expert bait fisherman than an expert fly fisherman or plug caster. It just looks easier, and that's what fools most people.

Worm fishing for trout isn't at all like pole vaulting or sword swallowing—you can't see at a glance what needs be done. It's almost as hard to discover what to do as it is to learn later how to do it. In short, it ain't easy to catch on to. Maybe "knack" is the only word for it, at that.

But even if the tricks of the bait-fishing trade are hard to define, this doesn't mean that they don't exist.

WORM FISHING

Let's first go back to an early June morning when I was a kid. The first rays of the rising sun find me perched on the end of a diving board over the ole swimmin' hole. I am engaged in a duel of nerves with a huge trout, his every spot visible through the crystal-clear water. In front of his nose hangs my worm-baited hook. Each time I try jigging it with my cane pole, the monster backs away. When I hold steady he creeps forward until only scant inches from the bait. He wants that worm. I earnestly want him to have it. Yet the old cuss won't take it—we just can't seem to get together.

I place the blame squarely on him. Doggone him, didn't I get there at daylight just to please him? Haven't I done everything that a human could do? Certainly I have. My conscience is clear.

Partly due to impatience and partly to the splinters that make themselves felt through the seat of my britches, I shift my position. The springy diving board dips, upsetting the open can of worms at my side. I catch the can with a quick grab, but too late—the contents already have spilled into the water. Down toward my trout drifts a veritable shower of worms. They stretch and squirm frantically, all plainly alive and full of pep. They settle slowly, naturally, neither restrained by a line nor dragged down by a heavy sinker and hook. Last but not least, they yield to the slow current and sink at just the correct downstream angle.

The trout's reaction is electrifying. Instantly he becomes a zooming, dipping form of fluid grace, banking and swirling to gobble worm after worm. Gone is his hesitation, his sense of caution. He darts after the last worm and snatches it just before it reaches bottom. Nothing remains in sight now but my baited hook. My scalp prickles and I clutch my pole, tense with anticipation. Surely, now, he'll take!

But wait, how can this be? Instead of racing in to collect this last tidbit, he edges toward it as cautiously as before—and halts! I jig my bait frantically (can't the fool see that here's another fat worm?). The trout turns scornfully and heads upstream, deliberately, without haste. His broad tail wags a final good-by as he disappears under the broken surface at the head of the pool. Thoroughly beaten, I hurl insults, and the empty worm can, after him and leave the scene in utter disgust.

There you have it—this matter of worm fishing. Here was a trout that asked for nothing better than a full meal of angleworms. He was hungry—on the feed. Nevertheless, he could not bring himself to tolerate the many suspicious aspects of my crudely presented bait. Had I known how to offer him a worm that looked and behaved as a worm should, I would have caught that trout!

But let's forget about this particular trout and see what you can do to make a worm on a hook behave like one that went out for a stroll and tumbled into the drink. Let's start with hooks, themselves, for they, at least, are pleasantly tangible and concrete.

Hooks

Suppose you sneaked up on a deep pool and tossed a loose worm into the run-in. If you hadn't been seen or heard, the first trout to spot the tumbling worm almost certainly would snap it up. Except for indigestion, he'd have no reason to do otherwise. Now, suppose you jab a large hook into the next worm and set it adrift with no line attached. Some trout in the pool probably would ignore the sprouting hook, as well as its dragging effect, and gobble the worm just the same. Others might dart in, nip at it, then drop it. But it's an even bet that at least half the trout in that pool would pass it up completely as just too darned suspicious-looking and -acting to monkey with. Finally, hang a third worm on a hook the same size, tie it to your leader and drift it into the pool. Lay you two to one that even the boldest fish in the pool would have nothing to do with this combination.

Back to the starting point again, but, when you try worm and hook this time, use a small one—a No. 12, let's say. Bet not one trout in ten would notice this small bit of steel when buried in a loose worm. Tie hook to leader and business falls off sharply, of course, but this time at least *one* of the trout in the pool probably would take it if you fished it craftily.

In other words, you needn't fool all the trout in each pool to fill a creel. If you can just tempt one, the job doesn't take long. Yet, if you start with a big, heavy hook, by the time you have added the necessary drag of leader, line, and sinker,

Worm rig: a nightcrawler lightly hooked on a small, un-snelled hook. Note placement of split shot.

you have branded your bait as a booby trap so plainly that your chances of hoodwinking that all—important lone fish go tumbling into the cellar.

So, one of the first tricks of worm fishing, and certainly the easiest, is to use small hooks. Let No. 8's be your largest and use these when you can get by with the least deception—early in the season, in roily water, and in the heavier currents of large streams. As things get tougher, scale down the size accordingly. Use 10's, 12's, and even 14's, as the water grows lower and clearer, the currents lighter.

Remember, now, we're talking about fooling trout into hitting, not about landing them. Naturally, you can't take the liberties with a heavy fish hooked on a No. 12 that you can when using a No. 2 or 4, yet there is this to be said in favor of small hooks, even in this respect: You know that you can't horse your fish, so you handle them with extra care and lose no higher percentage of hooked fish than before, possibly not as high. Result: more fish hooked, more landed—and more sport landing them.

One more tip on hooks: Steer clear of the snelled variety. Comparatively speaking, you pay a dickens of a price for them, but what do you get? A bulky, visible loop close to the hook where, of all places, you don't want it; a snell that almost never matches the diameter of your leader point; a permanent snell-to-hook hitch-up that wears with use and becomes untrustworthy.

Buy loose hooks and tie them directly to your leader with a Turle knot. Select those with hollow-ground points and turned-down eyes—the kind used in tying wet flies of good quality. Bought by the hundred they cost hardly more than a cent apiece, and they result in a much neater and stronger terminal rig. I like a plain round bend, but the clutching appearance of the Eagle Claw, or other models with rolled-in points, may give you a feeling of confidence. Small matter; they'll all hook and hold.

Sinkers

A free-drifting worm will sink to the bottom of its own accord, even in a strong current. If you can make your bait tumble along the bottom with no sinker at all, then do so by all means. Remember that a sinker is an added reason for suspicion in direct proportion to its weight. If you need help in getting the worm down, keep the amount of lead you use to a minimum. If tempted to pinch on a single split shot, try first with none at all. See if you can't persuade the currents to carry your bait close to the bottom. If, in heavier water, you feel you need a buckshot, see if you can make out with only a couple of small shot. Utilizing dropping currents to suck your worm down is one of the important tricks of the game. The less you need to rely on artificial weight, the better the results.

Baiting

If trout fed regularly on pretzels, then there would be at least some reason for looping a worm on a hook in the manner employed by many fishermen. To the contrary, however, trout expect worms to come tumbling along, writhing and stretching to gain a foothold that will help them to get out of their watery predicament. Baiting so your worm remains free to twist and squirm is a worming trick that's every bit as important as it is simple. Merely slide the barb of your small hook in, and out free, at a spot near the center of the worm. Only when lightly hooked in this manner can a lively worm advertise the freshness and vigor which are its chief selling points.

But remember this little baiting trick: In heavy currents a worm hooked in the middle tends to fold at the point of hooking with the two halves dragging downstream ahead of the hook. In such fast-water spots try hooking the worm through the "head" or tip. This lets it lie straight in the current, look more natural. Many times you can coax a strike from one of the faster bits of water by making this simple change. Don't worry too much about short strikes. If a trout decides he wants it, he'll usually take worm, hook and all at one gulp.

Light hooking is but part of the secret of baiting, however. Even when properly hooked, a worm soon becomes "drowned-out"—limp, lifeless, flavorless, and holding little trout-appeal in general. In spite of this it never seems to dawn on many fishermen that a fresh worm every few minutes brings far more bites.

You drift your bait, fresh and lively, into a promising hole. A trout sees it, wants it, but can't quite get up courage to tackle it. You run your bait through the hole time after time, for you know the value of thoroughness and patience. Your unseen fish remains interested and on the verge of taking, but by now your worm has grown a bit bedraggled and washed-out. You reach for another and hang it on the hook in place of the first. It squirms and wriggles from the shock of the hook and you hurry to fish it while it still writhes. This promptly tears it; your fish, already sorely tempted, can resist no longer when faced with a worm that now looks more inviting than ever, and he falls for the pitch. I wish I had a dollar for every trout I have taken by means of nothing more than this simple trick.

Just one more little hint about baiting: When you renew your bait, renew it completely. Strip the hook clean to avoid a gradual accumulation of faded, chewed-up bits of worm on the shank of the hook, which makes your bait appear just that much more unnatural and gives added reason for alarming a fish. Hook your worms lightly, change them often (and I mean *often!*), and keep the hook clean. These three easy-to-follow rules will bring you more trout.

Angleworms or Nightcrawlers?

Which makes the better bait, ordinary small garden worms or the big crawlers? Seems to me that the big worms have a bit more appeal for larger trout, a little less for run-of-the-stream fish. I expect this profound observation to win me few prizes; but, lest you accuse me of trying to capitalize on the obvious, I hasten to add that the difference isn't as great as one might suppose. Small worms will account for some mighty big trout, and little fellows will tackle crawlers with surprising audacity.

When streams run roily and the big ones are on the feed, though, I want my bait box filled with crawlers and nothing else. Under average conditions I like to have both along—small worms for the runs and riffles, and night-crawlers to try in every deep hole where I suspect a lunker may hide.

I have found one very real difference between these similar baits, however: it pays to fish more slowly when using the crawlers than when fishing the smaller worms. Trout seem to deliberate longer over the bigger baits—need less time to decide in favor of something smaller.

When it comes to fishing the crawlers in clear water, there's a trick that's so important—and little heeded—that I'm going to stick it in right here where it won't get mixed up with something else.

Draw a nightcrawler from your bait box and there you have a critter the size of a not-so-small snake. When you fish with crawlers, play it smart: drop down to your smallest hooks and a long, tapered leader. Here's your chance to effect such a contrast—big, attractive bait, light tackle—that the result is as close to perfect deception as you can come in bait fishing.

With small worms you hope the trout won't notice your tiny hook; with a nightcrawler they *can't* notice it, for you can hide it completely in the body of the bait! Much in the same way, the effects of a light, flexible leader are much less noticeable when the bait you tumble with the current is heavy and bulky. In other words, the big crawler appears very real, very substantial, very inviting—the artificial aspects of its hook-up trifling by comparison.

Fish nightcrawlers on your most delicate tackle, then, and you have one of the most killing big-trout baits you can drift into a pool! You also have the tip-off to all successful fishing tricks: increase the inducement, and at the same time do everything possible to reduce cause for suspicion to the vanishing point.

Leaders

I have just plugged a light leader as a distinct help in worm fishing. Now, permit me to reverse my field and say this: Don't make the mistake of overrating its helpful effect. A leader reduces the visibility of the mechanical connection between hook and line, but does a trout fear a line, anyway? I don't think so, at least not a line that merely dangles in the water. Remember my diving-board trout? He didn't hesitate to snap up loose worms all around the coarse line that hung from my cane pole. He refused to take my baited hook only because of its suspicious behavior. We know that it behaved oddly, neither sinking nor drifting downstream, because of the restraining influence of the line. I refuse to believe, however, that the trout "knew" this or was capable of "knowing" it. He simply didn't like the way the bait *acted;* that other thing that was my line didn't interest or influence him one way or the other.

For my money, then, a leader pays off in worm fishing mainly to the extent to which you utilize its flexibility, and the minimum resistance it sets up in the water, to drift your bait without drag (unnatural response to both currents and gravity). In other words, the finest leader serves little purpose if you let it hold your bait against the current when the laws of nature say that it should go tumbling downstream. Sure, the thin strand is next to invisible, but this sells no pencils as long as you allow the leader to have an unwholesome effect on your bait's behavior. Only when you fish with just the right amount of slack does your bait get that extra bit of freedom that a leader allows. Even then you aren't as far ahead of the game as some people would have you believe.

Please don't get me wrong. I wouldn't think of worm fishing for trout without a leader. For general fishing I like a six-foot strand of level nylon in six-pound test. For special purposes—the nightcrawler business is one example—I use a nine-foot leader tapered to 2X. I'm sure that with a leader I get a little better drift, and, in spite of what I have just said, the visibility factor lies in my favor for whatever it may or may not be worth. Just the same, insofar as worm fishing is concerned, this matter of leaders isn't the tree that holds the big coon. I'm certain of that, for I have had demonstrated all too forcefully the fact that it's possible to catch a lot of trout without using any leader at all!

The most expert worm fisherman I ever hope to know used a rugged bait-casting line and tied this directly to his hook. Sounds like a crude rig, maybe, but there was a fellow who could really catch trout. He'd pluck them from behind you and all around you, until you wondered what in the world ever gave you the idea you knew the first thing about trout fishing.

The trout certainly saw that black line of his, but so what? The worm would come trickling down a run with the line limp and slack, off to one side or behind—always where it couldn't influence the drifting bait. Worms come down the stream like that plenty of times, with maybe a wisp of weed or a sunken twig drifting alongside. But this black thing is a line? Phooey, who ever heard of a line? Wham!

I have given the subject of leaders this rather negative treatment deliberately, for it brings us face to face with the hard core of the worm fisherman's task: To fish his bait so that it rides the currents unhampered by the line (leader) to which it's tied.

Be a Rod-Tosser

Watch a fellow who really knows the business of worm fishing. I don't mean just anybody who fishes with bait and has run-of-the-mill luck. I mean a chap who takes trout you measure in pounds where most others catch fish a few inches over legal length. No such fellow? You just don't get around. Find that guy and watch him!

One thing you'll notice: he fishes a "live" rod. Always the tip of his rod is moving. Not much, maybe, but that constant slight motion holds the key to his success. Each little toss and flick of the rod gives his bait another free ride—causes it to drift naturally for that single moment that's all that's needed to bring a hit.

Let's say that you stand thigh-deep in the fast water above a likely pool. You have rigged up carefully and have a fresh, lively worm on your hook. Before you do another thing, strip plenty of slack from your reel and hold the loose coils in your free hand. This supply of slack is to be your ammunition in your coming fight against drag. Without it, you're licked before you start.

Okay, you're all set. Your first job is to have your bait close to the bottom when it rides into the pool—well sunk so the undertow can catch it and suck it down where the trout lie watching for food. Thus, you must drop your worm almost at your feet, or the fast current will carry it into the pool before it has time to settle. Right here we have one of the basic tricks of worm fishing: Always drop your bait well upstream from the spot that holds the trout. Elementary, to be sure, but I've watched too many fishermen ignore this one important little detail not to mention it. They start the

Downstream worm casting with no slack line

worm upstream a bit, yes, but they underestimate the speed of the current and seldom give the bait the time and distance it needs to sink to the fish-taking level.

Start your bait off as you should—in the fast flow well above the pool. Yes—but this doesn't guarantee anything. The fast current snatches the bait and, if you do nothing to prevent it, soon pulls the line taut. Your bait planes toward the top, just when it should drop into the depths, and this brings snickers from every trout in the pool. Here's where you must start working that rod.

To tumble downstream naturally your bait must have slack, but never too much at any one time. You toss the tip of your rod—waggle it up and down—and with each toss you slip just enough slack through the guides to match and rod. Why not dump all the slack on the water at once and have done with it? Doesn't work for one big reason. Bottom currents almost always are slower than those higher up. Faster water at the higher levels soon bellies the line out ahead of the bait and hurries the worm downstream at an unnaturally fast pace. More snickers from the trout!

Fish your bait on a slack line, but keep the slack always behind the bait! This is the wood that really makes shingles—the one worming trick that puts more trout in the creel than all the others combined. Not as simple as it sounds, for you're

Downstream worm casting with too much slack.

always busy striking the proper balance. Only by keeping the tip of your rod gently rising and falling can you sense whether to feed a bit of slack or to regain a trifle. Here's how to work it:

You lift the tip—flick it upward, really—with a short, quick wrist motion. If the line tightens against the bait (or sinker, if any) you can feel it through the sensitive tip—or learn to. The instant you feel this slight resistance, you let a little slack slide through your fingers. You do it quickly, automatically, releasing the slack before the rod can lift the bait or yank it against the current.

If you feel nothing but the line, then you know that you have regained slack that probably has been carried on ahead of the bait. You drop the tip for the next toss, and this deposits the retrieved bit of slack behind the bait where it belongs. You keep tossing, but you release no more slack until again you feel the direct pull of the bait.

Keep in mind that we're talking in terms of mere inches of line and tiny flicks of the rod. To do any good these hitches have to come fast—at least one to the second, I should say. That's why some expert worm fishermen give the impression that they're merely jigging the bait. They aren't! They're working on that line, mending and nursing it along so that it interferes as little as possible with the drift of the worm.

Downstream worm casting with controlled slack.

It takes practice to develop a feel for this subtle technique, but you've taken the biggest jump when you concede that possibly it exists and is worth trying. Can I prove that it does? Well, some people are mighty hard to convince. But show me a fellow who fishes a worm on a "dead" rod, and I bet I can dig up a real worm fisherman who'll catch two trout to his one, and probably twice as big. He'll do it because he has taken pains to learn how to control his line to produce the least drag. And he'll do *that* by pecking away constantly with the sensitive tip of his rod!

But why so fussy? Trout aren't overburdened with brains, so why should they give a hoot how a worm behaves, so long as it's fresh and full of flavor? Look at it this way: At least they expect familiar objects to respect and obey the physical laws of their medium, just as we look for them to honor those of ours. Suppose a waiter brings you a prime, juicy steak. He places the plate in front of you, but the steak refuses to follow it all the way to the table. It hovers in mid-air several inches above the crockery! Would you ask no questions and calmly ply knife and fork? Or would you promptly come down with a bad case of nerves?

You offer a trout the same cause for alarm when you fish a worm with pronounced and uninterrupted drag—a worm that rises when it should sink, hangs to one spot when it should tumble along downstream, or races faster than the particular current that carries it. Kill that drag with behind-the-bait slack. See if you don't fool more trout!

Look Things Over

No two pools, runs, or pockets are identical. Take a good look at each one before you fish it. Size up the situation in terms of likely currents and potential hiding spots, and start your bait on its way only after you have set a pattern for its behavior that will be natural for that particular place and, therefore, acceptable to the trout. Locate the hot spots— the pay-dirt areas—and concentrate on them. If tricky currents force you to compromise, destroy the illusion of free drift above these spots whenever drastic line correction is required to tumble the bait naturally through the promising areas. This ability to sense when to relinquish all pretense of deception, in order to regain it at just the proper time to encourage a strike, is one of the most valuable and difficult tricks of the trade.

Where the Heck Are They?

Half the battle is won if you can sense with accuracy just where the trout are likely to be. Remember that a feeding trout generally chooses a station which meets these three requirements:

1. It affords cover or concealment.
2. It permits examination of an important current.
3. It provides a cushion of "easy" water which allows the fish to stay put with a minimum of effort.

These three requirements can be met in an endless variety of ways, and it is up to you to recognize them wherever they occur in combination.

Look at the backwater in a large pool. Note that its slow, rotary current does not overlap the sweep of the channel; debris caught in the backwater will circle for hours. A trout can loaf against the mild push of the backwater while the main flow of the stream sweeps food in front of his very nose. Cover? Depth of water, alone.

A smooth slick looks barren of fish, but there is a large boulder on the stream bottom. A cushion of easy water exists around the entire boulder—in front of it, behind it, and along each side. Look for trout there, for they like to lie in the protecting shadow and watch for food in the water passing over them.

Sunken logs, overhanging branches, undercut banks, broken water surfaces, all afford cover for trout, so fish them carefully if they are near, or in, the main flow of the stream.

During the hot spells watch for the tiny inlets which signify springs. Trout, especially brookies, flock to the spring holes in midsummer, so be on the watch for these spots. Water dripping from an overhanging bank may be icy cold and attract fish. Drift your worm through these places whenever you find them.

Easy Does It

Patience in worm fishing is a virtue beyond measure. Trout, especially the big fellows, are not to be hurried. More than one fisherman has left a pool or run when one more drift of the worm would have brought the trout of his dreams. Fish slowly—do your worming at a worm's pace.

MINNOW FISHING

Set a minnow trap in a trout stream, and everything you find in it the next morning will be trout bait. Shiners, striped dace, small suckers, and chubs—you can use all of these with good results along with any other species of small-bait fish native to the stream. If you have a choice, settle for shiners, for they seem to hold a slight edge. Not much, though.

Found in many Eastern trout streams is an excellent little bait fish that I know by no name other than "chuckle-head." This homely little chap looks like a miniature cross between a bullhead and a sculpin, but the trout are more than tolerant of his appearance. He hangs to the bottoms of small, cold streams where his coloration of mottled muddy-gray makes him hard to distinguish, though he can be captured quite easily in a small dip net once he has been located. It is always a bother to catch a supply of these little fellows, but there is no finer trout bait.

Dead or Alive

Unlike most game fish, trout seem to find a dead minnow as attractive as a live one and, if anything, prefer the former. I sometimes buy bait from a dealer who keeps his minnow boxes in a pool inhabited by a dozen big brook trout. These trout are not confined, but chose to remain in the pool to receive daily handouts of dead minnows as the dealer cleans his boxes. Feeding on little else, some of these trout have grown well into the three-pound class. This taste for dead minnows makes it unnecessary to keep the bait alive on the stream, and simplifies minnow fishing considerably.

Drift a dead minnow downstream or cast it up and across and let it float back, and it will produce fish. Work it in the current with a slow, erratic spin and you have added flash and action which will call trout from a greater distance and provoke more strikes. To make a minnow spin, it should be "sewn" on the hook.

Sewing Class

For best results you need an eyeless, short-shank snelled hook—No. 4 is about right—with the snell soaked for pliability if it is of gut. Run the point down through the lower jaw of a dead minnow and draw the hook through and clear, along with a few inches of snell. Thrust the point down through the top of the head and out at the bottom. Reverse the hook (point it toward the tail) and shove it into the side of the bait between dorsal fin and tail. Bring the point out near the back (it will point toward the minnow's head) and take up the slack in the snell, drawing the minnow's body into a curve which produces the spin. The more curvature, the faster the spin; a few experiments will disclose the proper amount.

With a baiting needle you can be real fancy with your stitching. File an opening in the lower part of the eye of a large darning needle, and catch the loop of the snell in the opened eye. Run the needle under the skin of the bait near the tail and bring it out halfway toward the head. Draw the snell up until the shank of the hook has been pulled under the skin and shove the needle straight through the minnow at the halfway mark. Pull the snell after it and drive the needle back through the bait just behind the gills. Insert the point in the gill opening and push it up through the top of the head and complete the job by coming down through the lower jaw. Tighten the snell to give the desired degree of curve.

With a sewn minnow you can fish a drifting bait or you can spin it in the current. Best results are obtained by interweaving the two methods. Allow the minnow to tumble with the current until it is near the bottom, then hit it softly with the rod a few times to spin it and to start it toward the top. The action is likely to attract a trout and, if he doesn't strike promptly, he may gather the bait in as soon as you allow it to settle once more.

Always place swivels ahead of a sewn minnow, else your line will become hopelessly twisted.

More Minnow Business

You won't always have minnows along with you on the stream, but here's a stunt which sometimes helps to compensate when you need them.

Examine the trout you catch and you'll find an occasional trout with a minnow in its mouth, or part way down its throat. What better proof do you want that here, indeed, is a good bait? Put that very minnow to use in the next few pools. This trick seldom fails to produce a strike, probably because minnows aren't found in trouts' mouths unless they are feeding on minnows at the time, that particular kind and size.

Tiny minnows, less than two inches long, are excellent bait. Hook these little fellows through both lips with a No.-10 hook and make them dart just under the surface by

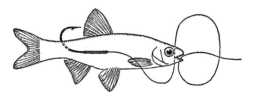

Correct method of sewing minnow bait.

twitching them against the current. There'll be a swirling rise whenever they're taken.

Hook your chuckleheads—if you can get them—in the same manner, but try and work them deeper as they're strictly bottom-dwellers. A trout that turns down a chucklehead is just plain off his feed.

Fishing a minnow behind a spinner is good business, especially early in the season when cold water makes the trout somewhat sluggish. In this case it is best that the minnow swim naturally, so rig up two tandem hooks in the same way that you made your worm gang. Hook the forward hook through both lips of the minnow and bind the trailing hook to the minnow's body with thread or secure it with a tiny rubber band. Precede the bait with a No. 4 June Bug spinner, and you may hook something you'll remember for the rest of your days.

If whole minnows go untouched, cut one in half and fish the tail section as you would a bucktail or streamer. It sometimes makes the sun break through the dark clouds.

Cannibals

Did you ever catch a seven- or eight-inch trout with match-ing "crimp" marks on opposite sides of its body? Don't let such marks pass unnoticed, for they are the jaw marks of an old lunker and the trout which bears them is alive only by a miracle. You can be sure that the big meat-eater lives in a nearby pool, probably the largest, so don't fail to give him your best treatment.

The biggest brown trout I ever hooked—and I lost him—was just such a cannibal who reared up and struck just after I had caught a brookie wearing the indelible stamp of his jaws. Needles to say, minnows are the things to offer these big, fish-hungry babies.

Dark of the Moon

Do you have a burning desire to catch a really large trout? Instead of answering so foolish a question, go get a few four-inch minnows, some 2/0 hooks, heavy sinkers, some ten-pound test nylon, your usual fishing equipment . . . and a flashlight. Wait until evening and then set out for a stream known to hold big trout. Pick the most likely pool you know—if it is one from which you have never been able to take a fish, so much the better, for that's a good sign it's the domain of one or more old busters.

Tie three feet of the heavy nylon to your line and rig it with big hook and sinker. Pass the point of the hook through the mouth of a dead minnow and out a gill opening. Draw the hook clear and shove the point under the dorsal fin, making sure that the barb comes free. Now you're ready for business.

Disregard the head of the pool and concentrate on a quiet backwater or eddy. Under cover of darkness, the big boys feel safe to come out of hiding and cruise the quiet water for minnows. If you've never seen them, you'll just have to take my word for it.

Pick out a spot and cast your minnow well out into the pool. Prop your rod in a forked stick and strip plenty of loose line from the reel, coiling it on the ground under the rod. Now light your pipe and take it easy.

Have no fear that your minnow, lying stiff, stark, and motionless on the bottom, will fail to attract the attention of the first big trout to cruise nearby. He'll pick it up, but it may be some little time before he happens along. If you are inclined toward impatience, remember that the stakes are high.

With the first swish of line whipping through the guides, thrust down your rising excitement and pick up your rod, taking care to put no strain on the line. Let the fish move off as far as he likes; he'll stop presently to swallow the minnow. Give him ample time to get the bait down—at least a couple of minutes—then strip slack with the rod held low, until you can feel the fish with the tip. Make sure that the line is taut against the trout, then drive that big hook home as though you meant business.

What you do next is up to you . . . and the trout. If you've never played a heavy fish in pitch darkness, you're in for a brand new experience.

Check local laws to make sure that you are within legal fishing hours.

Wait Them Out

Minnow fishing is predominantly big-trout fishing, so work with extreme thoroughness and patience. A huge trout may resist capture for years and then fall to someone who was willing to work on him for just a little longer than anybody else cared to. Steel yourself against long, dull periods between strikes by remembering that your rewards will come in big hunks if you keep at it.

À LA CARTE

I once surprised a large brookie chewing on a side of bacon which apparently had turned rancid and had been cast into the stream. On another occasion I watched with lifted hackles while a pair of tremendous rainbows tore the overripe body of a huge rat to bits and devoured it with obvious relish. I recommend neither rancid bacon nor defunct rats as bait, but these incidents point to surprising range in trout appetites and infinite bait possibilities.

For a variety of effective baits, there's no handier source than the shorelines of the streams you fish. Turn over rocks at the water's edge and you'll find them.

Salamanders

Not newts, which have little value as trout bait, but those lively, wriggling little chaps with bodies hardly larger than matchsticks. If you can catch one of these little wrigglers—you have to move fast—hook him through the lips without delay and drift him through the nearest pool before his wriggling subsides. He won't live long if there are trout around.

These little salamanders take first place on a trout's list of tidbits. In addition to being relished, they are relatively rare, which serves to make them doubly desirable. You don't often find one in a trout's stomach, but you'll seldom fail to get an enthusiastic strike when you use one as bait.

And Hellgrammites

Don't overlook these ugly larvae. In the cold water of trout streams they don't grow to be the big, leathery cusses generally used as bass bait, and are all the more attractive for their small size. Whenever you turn up one of these little trout-stream hellgrammites, hook it lightly under the collar and fish it as you would a worm. It's a good bait.

I remember one instance when a tiny specimen produced two successive rainbows in the pound-and-a-half class as quickly as I could place it in the water. How much longer *that* would have kept up I'll never know, for the second trout tore the hellgrammite loose and no amount of searching would turn up another.

And Just About Everything

You'll turn over hardly a rock without finding some sort of stream-side life. Nymphs of all kinds will cling to the bottom of each overturned stone, and one that you possibly can hold on a small hook is well worth trying.

Even the common earthworms found in this manner will have a freshness and flavor impossible to retain for any length of time in a bait box. Use them at once, for they probably will prove more attractive than those you have brought with you.

Be a rock-turner-upper. If anything moves, grab it and hang it on your hook!

Five, Six, Pick Up Sticks

"Stick worms"—larvae of the caddis fly—are common to trout streams and gain their name from their ability to sheathe themselves with bits of wood until they resemble sunken twigs resting on the bottom. Stripped of their cases, these larvae are looked on with high favor by trout.

Gather a supply of these caddis worms—you can pick them up almost anywhere along a stream—and drop them in your bait box. Rig up with tapered leader (3X is none too fine) a No.-14 hook of light wire and give your line a coating of grease to make it float. Draw one of the tiny worms from its case, thread it carefully on the hook, and fish it upstream, exactly as you would a dry fly.

Cast delicately to keep the worm on the hook, and drop it near the head of a pool. Strip slack as the line floats toward you and watch for a check which will signal a strike. Hit the fish gently out of respect for your fine terminal tackle.

Caddis worms are especially effective during those periods of low, clear water when bait fishing is bound to be difficult. Fish them downstream if the overhang won't permit casting, but have at it in the upstream direction whenever possible.

Buzz, Buzz

The next time a formation of June bugs dive-bombs your screen door or window, go out and collect a supply of these hard-shelled beetles. Cast one upstream on a No.-10 hook and it will come floating back like a tiny brown test to their effectiveness.

How about houseflies and the big bluebottles? Trout love them. They require a tiny hook and they won't stand much casting but you can float them downstream or dap them over the grass-hung banks of meadow streams.

Don't overlook the insects which hatch along the streams—the May flies or drakes. They are difficult to put on a hook and to handle, but they can be put to good use with a little ingenuity. Many times a favorable breeze can be utilized to carry them over a pool and dance them along the surface. They will be taken avidly.

Bees and hornets probably would work well, but that's where I draw the line.

Hippity Hop

Grasshoppers leap first and look afterward, and are forever plunking down in trout streams. During the late summer months trout gobble them by the thousands and are just begging to be tricked by a juicy hopper on a small hook.

As is to be expected, trout will rise with enthusiasm to a grasshopper fished on the surface. Oddly enough, they also produce well when fished deep, so try both methods to see which works the better.

Grasshoppers are difficult little cusses to control when carried alive. If you do as I do, you'll execute them as you catch them by nipping their heads between the nails of thumb and forefinger. Given this treatment, they'll stay put in the bait box and, as far as I can tell, will be every bit as attractive to the trout.

Crickets are on a par with grasshoppers, though more care must be taken to keep them on the hook. Lay in your supply in the early morning while the dew is still on the grass. They don't like moisture and will be found congregated under old boards and loose rocks where the ground is dry.

Those big locusts which flush ahead of you like timber-doodles are fine for trout, although they are difficult to catch. Place one on a small hook and give him a gentle toss with the rod. If you're lucky, he'll land in the water with wings beating.

Don't waste time on a trout who refuses a fluttering locust; he's neurotic and at odds with the world.

In Short

There's little in the way of living tissue which trout won't accept in one form or another, so be as democratic in your offerings as they are in their tastes. Here's one more little dodge which may whet their appetites:

Rig up with a worm gang and bait the first hook with a cricket or grasshopper, the second with a small hellgrammite or worm and the tail hook with a minnow tail. What more can they ask—a printed menu?

POND AND LAKE FISHING

This is a complete subject but I intend to penetrate it only to the depth of a few basic hints. Let's start with brook trout.

Ponds

Pond brookies can be taken early in the season by dangling a worm almost anywhere. Come warmer weather, and they retreat to the spring holes and become shy and selective to the point of exasperation. Locate these hangouts by exploring the deepest sections of the pond and any inlets which may bring cold water.

Nymphs and larvae such as the caddis worm, hellgrammite, dragonfly nymph, etc., are among the better baits and will generally outproduce worms. Fish them with a fine tapered leader, small hook, and *no sinker*. Make as long a cast as possible and let your bait settle to the bottom and remain undisturbed for several minutes. If it is not taken, start it along the bottom in tiny hitches by retrieving line with a very slow hand twist. Continue with your twist retrieve until the nymph reaches the very top of the water. Trout may follow it along the bottom without taking, and then grab it on the way to the surface.

If you take my advice, you'll leave the ponds alone after streams. If you're a stubborn cuss, use the finest possible tackle, effect a slow, natural motion of the bait, and feed them tidbits rather than full dinners.

Lakes and Lunkers

Trolling is a standard method for taking those big browns and rainbows—brookies too, if they are present. Troll near the surface in early season and deep when the water has warmed. A sewn minnow makes a good trolling lure, or you can run it behind a spinner arrangement. The latter can range from a single blade to the Dave Davis rig which consists of spinners in tandem to give off a maximum of flash and glitter.

Nightcrawlers trolled behind a spinner or spoon work well in lakes and here is a simple and effective rig for their use:

Remove the hooks from a large red and white casting spoon and replace them with a worm gang of No.-6 hooks whipped to a 15-inch snell. Drape a crawler on the gang and troll at a speed which will give the spoon a slow wobble.

Such spoons are effective when used without bait and, for an interesting variation, try trolling a tiny red and white spoon a foot or so behind one of the large ones. Be sure to use swivels ahead of all trolling rigs.

Still fishing pays off if you have the patience to sweat them out. Nightcrawlers fished just off the bottom are always a good bet, as are live minnows. Dead minnows are sometimes better. Let these rest on the bottom but jig them frequently to attract attention.

Some fishing tricks fail to make sense on the face of them, yet come through with flying colors when you can bring yourself to put them to the test. Here's one of that type to try on those sly browns and rainbows that have grown fat and heavy by turning down all conventional baits.

Select one of your largest minnows and cut it in half. Take the tail-half and peel the skin back to the base of the tail. Slit the skin lengthwise several times so that it hangs from the body of the bait in narrow ribbons or streamers. Run your hook through the fleshy end and lower the bait close to the bottom.

Jig gently with the rod for several moments to make the shreds of skin flutter and wave. After a few minutes of jig-ging, drop the minnow tail to the bottom and let it lie there. If nothing takes it at the end of five minutes or so, start it up and jig some more.

You may have to work a long time for your fish, but, when he comes, he's likely to be an old lunker too wise to fool with a plain minnow!

As a day-in, day-out proposition, bait fishing for trout in lakes shapes up as a sit-and-wait deal that takes a little too much patience for most of us. Fish, when you hook them, are likely to run big indeed, but it can be a long time between bites—and generally is. There is, however, one way to lick this. Pay no attention to lakes except on those relatively few days when conditions are ripe for a killing.

Pick only those days during or following a heavy rain. Rain, no matter how violent, has little effect on a lake of any size, but the tributaries—ah, a different matter entirely! Each

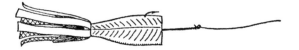

How to prepare a skinned minnow for lake fishing

swollen brook pours a steady stream of rain-washed food into the lake, and the trout gather at the mouth of each to feed. If you can contrive to be at one of these inlets when the stream is on the rise, you'll catch those usually stand-off-ish browns, rainbows, or squaretails with their guard down. Anchor where the roil mixes with the clear lake water, and lower a lively nightcrawler. Things should start happening in a matter of minutes!

UNCLASSIFIED

Which means a few rag-tag observations. The first one is plain screwy.

Watch Out Behind You

As a youngster I swam with my contemporaries in a pool below the remains of an ancient wooden dam. When we were through swimming, we would rush for our alder poles and catch trout, almost before the ripples had died away. It

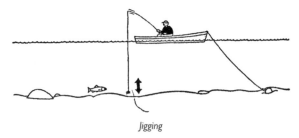

Jigging

sounds crazy, but our thrashing around seemed somehow to stimulate the trout and prompt them to bite.

I honor this early experience by casting behind me frequently, and it pays off often enough to keep me at it. I remember one 14-inch brookie which snapped up my worm the instant it landed in my muddy wake. It was the only decent trout taken over an entire day by three fishermen.

By a Waterfall

You can pick up bonus fish cram-jam against the base of a falls too high for trout to ascend. If the water falls to a flat shelf and then drops into a pool, fish the pool, but don't fail to try the shelf, no matter how barren it looks. There will be one or two trout hugging the foot of the falls if there is water enough for them to swim. You might as well have them as the next fellow.

Change of Pace

Thinking back over a lot of trout fishing on a good many streams, one trick keeps popping up as a tide-turner—the quick shift. You're having better-than-average luck with a certain bait or lure. Then you come to a likely pool where you get nary a nudge, although common sense tells you should connect. Finally, as a last resort, you try something radically different. One cast—bango!

This is an altogether different matter from changing lures when the fish aren't hitting. It involves removing a lure that has been producing steadily in favor of something untried. Generally the temptation to move on to the next bit of water wins out and you don't go to the bother of changing. You may pass up the prize of the day, however.

This has happened to me too many times to count it as coincidence. The way they slam into that second lure on the first cast indicates a cause-and-effect answer, and here's how I have it doped:

First, you hit on something that produces, something that packs a lot of appeal on that particular day. Several fish take it greedily, then you come to a spot that holds a customer with a bit more will power. Like the others, he wants your offering—maybe comes within an ace of grabbing it—but his super sense of caution holds him back. Such a fish, nevertheless, already wavering on the brink of decision, is now a better prospect than when you first walked up on him. Maybe he can resist the appeal of that first lure indefinitely, but when temptation unexpectedly appears in a second form it may prove to be just too much to bear. Thus, he's likely to bang whatever else you toss at him—almost anything, just so it's different. It's really nothing more than the old one-two punch; you set him up with the first lure, then come up from the floor with the crusher.

The tough part about this trick is that it calls for changing lures when probably you have but to move to the next hole to take a trout with what you already have on. Remember, though, that the hard-to-tempt fish live longest, grow the biggest. A change at the right time often raises one of these lunkers!

That Swimmin' Hole Trout

Remember him? Here's the trick I'd use to show him where lightning struck the barn.

I'd get a fat nightcrawler, and I don't think I'd use a hook a bit bigger than a No. 14. I'd rig it with at least a six-foot leader, then I'd get real cagey and pinch on a couple of buckshot, or a good-sized clamp-on sinker, *just below where the leader joined the line.* I'd flip this into the pool, let the sinker plunk to the bottom on a slack line, then barely tighten the line against the weight of the lead. In the meantime, the crawler would work downstream very slowly in the slight current until the leader was fully extended. It would then appear to lodge, which would be perfectly natural in a deep, quiet pool. The leader would lie along the bottom and have no apparent effect on the bait.

Once settled, I'd let the crawler lie there on the bottom and wriggle until the trout grabbed it. Bet he'd do it, too; maybe not right away, but eventually. The falling sinker and line would not disturb him as much as you might think—not enough to keep him from scooping up a worm that lay a good six feet from these objects and seemed in no way associated with them.

It boils down to the fact that in deep, quiet pools of glass-clear water, the only place to fish a worm is smack on the bottom. You can't make it look and behave as it should in any other way—line and leader always affect it seriously if you try to sink it slowly, and to let it dangle at some arbitrary depth is a worse giveaway. Get it right down on the gravel, and keep the sinker a full leader-length away from the worm!

Robinson Crusoe

He lived on an island, didn't he? This is about islands—the little islands in trout streams.

Ever notice that these little plots of high ground never split the stream equally in half? Which way to go? Follow the main current as other fishermen would? Aha! As other fishermen would, eh? Maybe the smaller branch hasn't been fished for a month.

Go around the "poor" sides of those little islands. You'll pick up more than one good trout doing just that.

Spotted Trout

Any fisherman worthy of the name is always on the watch for trout, whether he be fishing or less sensibly employed. Here's a trick which will help you to "spot" trout, and that should lead to taking them.

Pick up a thin piece of shale or slate the size of a dime and flick it into a quiet pool. Watch it twinkle and spin as it slants toward the bottom. Note how its progress can be followed far into the green depths. Note also, you lunkhead, that a two-pound trout has just made a pass at it! How long is it going to take you to get back there with a rod?

Another way to count noses is to inspect streams when the fall spawners (brookies and browns) are on their spawning beds. Look for the browns in the riffles of the main stream where bright areas of freshly turned gravel betray their presence. Search for spawning brook trout in the headwaters.

You may be astounded by what you see—especially in "fished-out" streams. Though your hands will be tied at the moment, the knowledge that those trout are there should provide that extra margin of strength and courage which you need to live through a long, dull winter.

2. Fly Fishing

NOWADAYS WE TAKE FLY FISHING AND FLY FISHER-men pretty much for granted. I can remember when this was not the case. When you wanted a mess of trout you went at it in an honest, direct manner by first digging a can of worms. Fly fishing, what little was done, smacked strongly of the black arts—the seething caldron and witches' brew. People weren't quite sure that it was on the level.

Maybe I have exaggerated a little. I guess there were a few fellows around who took their trout on flies regularly and still were allowed in the barber shop. Try as I might, though, I could never catch them at it. A fellow tells me he likes fly fishing best because he gets the most sport from it, though, and I'm with him all the way. Trout *rise* to a fly—those fished on or near the surface, at least—and the sudden, flashing swirl of an old soaker is a thrill you seldom get in bait fishing. Then, too, fly-hung trout are almost invariably lip-hooked;

lightly stung by but a tiny barb, they can, and do, give you every ounce of fight they have in them.

DRY FLY FISHING

When you come right down to it, taking trout on a dry fly is about as simple a process as you can find in all fly fishing. Stream insects hatch, ride the surface film for a short time, and trout rise to snatch them before they can take to the air. Well-tied dry flies imitate these insects with enough realism to fool many waiting trout. You just float them among rising fish, give them no action, and let nature take its course.

Setting the hook is just as simple, for you can see the trout take your flies. To make it even easier, many trout hit with a clearly audible Kerwhoosh! You can put the hook to these with your eyes closed.

As simple and easy as all that? Well, not quite, maybe. Pin me down, and I'll have to admit that no fly fishing is simple. Right off the bat you can stump me with the following question.

What Are They Taking?

Some fishermen recommend an immediate autopsy of the first trout taken to determine stomach contents. Maybe this gets them somewhere, but, to me, this partly digested conglomeration generally looks like a mixture of old coffee grounds and sweepings from the floor of a covered bridge. And what should you use to catch that first trout? By the time I take him I've found the fly I'm looking for—the one I took him on!

But what *are* they taking? This is sometimes a vital question, but, more often, not nearly as important as many fishermen seem to think. A good share of the time the answer is: *anything and everything that looks good.*

I remember one morning of fast and furious dry-fly fishing when every trout I took was crammed with big, fat June bugs. I took every last one of them on a No. 14 Adams, a pattern and size that they hardly could have mistaken for a June bug. An abundance of food of one particular kind doesn't always mean that trout won't rise for something completely different if they get the chance.

It doesn't mean that they will, either, and this uncertainty helps to make dry-fly fishing the fascinating sport that it is. Sometimes they will accept nothing but a close imitation of some particular insect. Then you must try to "match the hatch."

Pattern

When trout show a rigid preference for a particular item it usually is due to a generous hatch of one of the common species of May flies. Sparse hatches of less common insects seldom result in such marked selectivity, and, when they do, they impose a problem so difficult that generally it's best left alone. First of all, it's difficult to identify the hatch in most cases. Then, if you finally succeed, you seldom have anything in your fly box that represents even a fair imitation. Or, if you do manage to come to some decision, by that time the hatch most likely is over and the rise a thing of the past.

At any rate, I prefer to try to match only the common May flies and let the rest go chase themselves, for I believe it results in greater over-all fishing efficiency. If you subscribe to this simplified approach, then you need worry about only a few basic patterns, for a mere half-dozen contain imitations of all the major hatches.

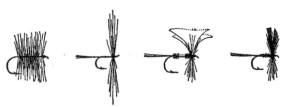

Four types of dry flies

Quill Gordon, Hendrickson, Red Quill, March Brown, Light Cahill, and Cream Variant—these patterns provide a choice that you will find adequate under most circumstances. The Hendrickson poses as *Ephemerella Invaria,* the Red Quill as *Ephemerella Inuaria,* female and male respectively of the same species. And, by copying from the same book, I could give you the low-down on the rest of them.

For our purpose, however, the trick is not that of identifying or classifying May flies by their scientific names, but merely in terms of which of our basic patterns they most closely resemble. With merely six patterns to chose from, you need waste no time in deliberation. If the hatch resembles the Quill Gordon a bit more than the Hendrickson, tie the Quill Gordon and go to it. If you can't decide which of two patterns comes closest to matching the fly coming off the water, then probably it doesn't make a bit of difference which you choose. In other words, by picking the most appropriate of these few dependables you can come up with a reasonably good imitation (about all you can hope for, anyway) with very little fussing around.

A good part of the time you won't need to worry about matching the hatch, however, for there will be no hatches in evidence. Then your job consists of pounding them up with no visible rises to aid you in locating fish.

You can use any old pattern for this, but some seem to have particular qualifications that recommend their use for "blind" fishing. Strangely enough, some of the best of these are patterns that look like no known insect, at least when viewed by human eyes. The Royal Coachman (both standard and fanwing), the various Wulff's, and the bivisibles typify this last group and are among its leading producers.

Spider patterns—short-shanked flies that feature little other than extremely long hackles—at times are especially effective in coaxing rises when no insects are on the water. An occasional smart twitch does no harm when fishing these flies, by the way.

Flies in which two contrasting shades of hackle are mixed—the Adams is an outstanding example—have a special appeal of their own and deserve high mention as persuaders. While tying my supply of Quill Gordons I always turn out a dozen or so in which I blend a brown hackle with the blue dun that the pattern calls for. These I reserve for hatchless periods, and they bring excellent results.

Actually, of course, there is no hard and fast rule about all this. A big, incongruous Royal Coachman Fanwing may do very nicely right at the height of a hatch (as indeed I shall relate) or a trout may come from out of nowhere to take a Quill Gordon. It's just that some patterns lend themselves a bit better to matching particular insects when this need exists; others, to probing for fish when no surface feeding is evident.

There is one trick that you should remember, however, that involves the deliberate use of a large, nonimitative pattern when flies *are* on the water. This, incidentally, brings up one more of the many mysteries of fly fishing.

Sometimes you will find the air filled with dancing May flies, the surface of the water covered with their floating bodies. This is not a hatch, of course, but the end of the trail. The flies dip down to deposit their eggs on the water then they promptly die. Usually there will be a few halfhearted rises—just enough to set you groping in your fly box for a matching pattern.

Although this is the natural move, it is a foolish one, nevertheless. Even should you come up with a perfect imitation, your fly will merely be one among many thousands with sweepstake odds against its being singled out. (There is never any such number of flies on the water during an actual hatch.) The real gimmick, however, is the strange and inexplicable fact that trout have little appetite for these spent spinners, as witness the listless, sporadic feeding in the midst of such plenty. No actual feeding at all, probably; more of a nosing-over process.

The smart caper here is to forget about duplicating the spent flies, and slip them something that will stand out from the crowd—a big bivisible, a Wulff, a Royal Coachman Fanwing. I have done this when the surface was almost a solid mat of dead flies and had my fly snatched from among the thousands of floating naturals on the first cast. Try it the next time you find the water covered with spent spinners—give them something different!

My advice to the contrary, I expect that a good many patterns will find their way into your fly boxes, just as they do into mine. Nevertheless, you need no more than a dozen (if that many) to take trout consistently. Make sure, however, that you carry duplicates of your reliables in a goodly variety of sizes.

Size

Trout quite probably refuse a dry fly because of its size far more frequently than because of its pattern. If we're honest, we'll admit that the majority of dry-fly patterns differ very little in appearance if we disregard the color factor, and it has never been established that trout can distinguish color in a floating fly. In spite of our beliefs and our experience-gained "evidence," we may be kidding ourselves about some patterns—the trout may not be able to tell one from the other.

Size variations, on the other hand, must be as apparent to them as to us, and, indeed, they at times give ample evidence that the size of a fly is a matter that they refuse to take lightly.

I believe that no preference for insects of a particular size determines the size of the fly you must use to take trout, but rather the clarity with which trout see the fly on the water. With this as my guide, the problem of what size fly to use becomes extremely simple—the slicker and slower the surface I'm fishing, the smaller the fly (and finer the leader) I use. And here's another trick:

Big hatches of big flies come early in the season—usually before the low-water period when fishing "fine and far off" is the accepted thing. Nevertheless, some of these hatches occur in smooth runs where the surface shows hardly a ripple. The flies are sizable, though—No. 12 in size, or even No. 10—so you string along with them in making your fly selection, and use a matching size. But no matter how carefully you fish among the rising fish, the answer is no.

Now try this: Stick to the same pattern, but scale it down to No. 14, or even to No. 16. Now your fly no longer matches the hatch in size, but neither does its every detail stand out through that limpid surface as did that of the larger one. The small fly does not pose as the genuine article, but neither does it flaunt glaring imperfections of disguise. It hints but with no guarantee; suggests but does not insist. *And to such items whose merits remain sufficiently problematical trout will rise!* This is the touch to try for in all dry-fly fishing, in fact, for few trout are fooled by flies they see in detail.

You can take trout on the larger flies at any time of year, just so long as one factor or another blurs their outline— a dancing surface, a wind ripple, or the black of night. By the same token, you'll have better luck with the tiny flies whenever and wherever you strike glassy-smooth water. Let conditions be your guide, not the size of the season.

Of course late-season fishing calls for small flies, but only because the water at that time almost always is low and clear. Sure, the trout feed on tiny insects then, but simply because the hatches run to smaller sizes—they'd take the big drakes and love them if only they'd hatch. So, even late in the summer, don't hesitate to use a fly of substantial size wherever you find broken water or whenever you fish after dark. Use the midges only when and where you must—during daylight hours; in the smooth flats and runs.

In my fly box I like a few No. 8's, a larger number of No. 10's, lots and lots of 12's and 14's, a fair number of 16's, and a few 18's. So armed, I'm ready to chuck a given pattern at them in any reasonable size. Makes sense, I *think*.

Dry-fly Quality

The best dry flies ride high on the water, supported only by their hackle tips and tail fibers (another help in breaking outline). Choose those that are tied on hooks of light, fine wire and with stiff, vibrant hackles. Place a fly on a book or other flat surface and hold it at eye level. If the hook touches the surface, the fly is either poorly tied or its hackles and tail fibers fail to meet dry-fly standards.

Leaders

To fool trout with a dry fly you need a long leader which tapers to a fine point. Most water calls for a length of at least nine feet, and to take fish from smooth, unbroken stretches you may have to go to 12 feet or more. The longer your leader the better, provided its length doesn't gum up your casting, so make it a point to use the maximum length practical for the water you fish. On big streams, for example, you can make long casts, and a leader as long as 15 feet will straighten out and fall extended—a decided help in deceiving the trout. Where you are restricted to short casts a 15-foot leader would be a hopeless handicap and you must settle for a shorter length.

A fine leader point not only reduces the visibility of the connection between your leader and fly; its flexibility allows the fly to respond in a natural manner to the impulses of the current—an absolute essential in trout deception. Use leader points (tippets) no heavier than 3X for your Nos. 12 and 14 dry flies, and drop down to 4X and 5X strands when you switch to the tiny sizes.

And Fish Them Just So

If more fly fishermen had fished seriously with natural baits, I suspect that there would be less frantic searching for just the right pattern of fly, more concentrating on technique. The fellow who uses bait soon learns that there's a great deal more to trout fishing than merely convincing fish that you have some genuine article of food on the hook. In bait fishing, in fact, this problem doesn't exist at all—you offer not a close imitation, but the real thing. Nevertheless, you still have to fish just as craftily to take any appreciable number of trout.

If exact duplication of this, that, or the other were the whole answer, think what you could do with live grass-hoppers at the height of the hopper season—probably take every trout you came to. You couldn't help it, for what comes closer to matching a grasshopper than another grass-hopper? It never works that way, though. Although hoppers make attractive trout bait, you fool only a small percentage of the trout you try them on, just as you do when using any other bait or lure.

Probably every trout knows instinctively that your bait is an honest-to-goodness grasshopper and therefore good to eat. Why, then, do so many of them decide to leave it strictly alone? They don't like the way the thing *acts*, that's why. In the case of the few you take, you probably manage just the right drift of the hopper at the crucial time. To these fish the grasshopper not only looks real but *behaves* as it should, in a natural manner. So, they go for it.

The more you pry into the private lives and affairs of trout, the more evidence you find that they are extremely critical of a lure's behavior, care *relatively* little for its appearance.

So, when all's said and done, how you fish a fly has far more to do with results than the type of fly you use—and that's not discounting the considerable importance of the fly itself. If your technique is not lacking, then you'll take your share of trout on almost any fly you care to use. If you permit it to drag suspiciously, then I challenge you to discover a pattern that will compensate for this error. If you combine smooth technique with intelligent choice of pattern and size, then, of course, you really begin to go places. But, always, your technique counts most. Drag, often so slight that you can't detect it, will probably account for more refusals than all other reasons combined.

A fly cast directly upstream usually has the least tendency to drag. Fly, leader, and line drift back toward you at speeds so nearly identical that the fly drags but little, and perhaps not at all. As we shall see, however, casting directly upstream is not the wisest strategy, nor would it be possible to limit yourself to such casts even if they were the most desirable. To reach rising fish and likely spots you must cast upstream and across a good share of the time. This puts your line across currents flowing at different rates of speed, and the resulting tugging and hauling on your floating line soon causes your fly to drag (move more slowly or rapidly than the current that carries it, or cut across this current at an unnatural angle).

Since these varying currents are a constant factor in stream fishing you almost never can succeed in getting long, drag-free floats. Luckily, you do not need to. A smooth float of six feet is wonderful. One of 12 inches is enough to bring a strike, if it occurs just as the fly comes over the fish. One of the big tricks of dry-fly fishing, then, is shooting for as many of these brief intervals of drag-free float as you possibly can manage.

A slack line cast

Lay a straight, taut line across several currents and your fly drags almost instantly. This cheats you of what should have been a moment or two of free-drift and a good chance of a rise. Instead of trying to straighten out your casts prettily, try dropping a line that's somewhat on the loose and wavy side. You'll find that while the twists and bends are working out of the line your fly will float relatively free of drag. Let's hope a trout takes it.

If not, the fly will drag as soon as the line tightens against it. Should you pick it up and cast again? Not if you can squeeze additional floats from your original cast. Try "mending" your line: Raise your rod smartly, then flip a dose of slack into the line with a quick, but slight, roll cast. Done adroitly, this disturbs the fly hardly at all, and by redistributing your line on the water you give it another unbroken ride. "Mend" as many times as serves any purpose.

This trick of making the most of each cast is fully as important in dry-fly fishing as casting accurately in the first skillfully you dropped the fly. You can, of course, "mend" a cast in a hundred-and-one different ways. Your fly trickles around the base of a boulder perfectly, for example, but promptly drags in the backwater below. A quick lift of the rod skates it from the spot where it can do no good and drops it on another current where it gets a second chance to drift. As soon as it drags, another flick of the rod may put it in business again, and so on.

The thing to remember is that you can't afford to let your fly float willy-nilly, once you set it down. At the first sign of drag, destroy the pattern of your floating line to remove tension on the fly. At the same time try to guide the fly into a less troublesome current whenever there is the opportunity to do so. Make a play for a strike, write it off if it fails, then quickly make another. The more real bids you make per cast, the more trout you'll succeed in bringing up.

Keep the Line Off Them!

You see a trout rise. A rising trout is a feeding trout; serve him a fly attractively and the chances are better than fair that he takes it. Put your fly above the fish where it can drift down to him, and keep your leader and line to one side where he won't see them. Easy, if the trout lies across stream from you; cast to float the fly over his nose and line and leader fall between you and the fish.

Suppose you have no way of reaching him other than by casting directly upstream? Drop your fly above him, and the line plunks down across his nose. Trout, feeding trout especially, dislike this.

Pitch Him a Curve

A slick trick! Line and leader fall to one side of the fish while the fly loops around to settle directly upstream from him.

Curving your fly to the right is far easier than bending it around to the left, and shouldn't give you serious trouble—at least most fishermen can learn to do it. By casting

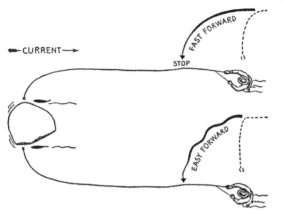

Left-hand curve cast (top) and right-hand curve cast (bottom)

side-arm—rod held well to the right of perpendicular—and allowing the line to fall to the water before it straightens, you can get the desired effect. Make your backcast with full power, but halt your forward thrust to cheat the line of the momentum needed to snap it straight or extend it completely.

To throw a curve to the left, cant the rod to the right as for the right curve, but put plenty of energy into your forward cast. Check the line sharply at the limit of the cast, and the fly *should* snap around to the left. That's the theory behind it, anyway, and maybe you can learn to pull the stunt off whenever you have need for it.

Curve casting is a trick worthy of your best efforts, and you stand to gain by practicing it. Fortunately you don't have to produce sharp, abrupt curves to benefit. If you can succeed in bending your fly only a little to the right or left, it helps that much in keeping line and leader hidden from the fish. This makes all the difference in the world to our present generation of gut-shy fish.

Where Did He Rise?

A fish leaves an expanding ring of waves when he rises, but in the current of a stream this ring refuses to stay put. It immediately starts drifting downstream, leaving you with no way of telling the trout's true position. If you yield to the natural tendency, the drifting ring will mislead you into dropping your fly on the trout's nose or behind him, instead of above him where it belongs.

The next time you cast to a rising fish, try this trick: Ignore the ring—the trout is no longer under it—and line up the rise immediately with some handy object on the opposite shore. Now you know exactly where the trout lies and you can take your time to pick the proper spot for your fly to drop—sufficiently upstream from the fish so that the fall of line and leader will not alarm him. Even if you fail to raise him, you can come back and work him over later on, for trout tend to hang to one spot for as long as they continue on the feed.

Fish Out the Float

If a trout doesn't take, let your fly float well past him before you pick it up. For all you know, he's drifting along under it just on the verge of rising. Or, if he lets it float past him, you'll give him the jitters by lifting the fly while it remains in his range of vision. Don't let him see it fall, and don't let him

How to fix the location of a rising trout

see it leave the water. A dozen floats without disturbance may be the only trick needed to coax a rise from him.

Be a Slowpoke

Don't let a rise in the next bend upstream put you in a sweat to get a fly over the fish as quickly as possible; try to remember that he'll keep until you can get to him in due course. Rush off upstream toward him, and you'll probabl frighten fish in the intervening water which you might have had for the asking. Worse yet, your hasty approach is bound to alarm the fish you saw rise before you get within casting distance and put him off his feed for the time being. It doesn't pay to hurry; slow-and-easy takes trout.

Skittering Fly

Skittering a dry fly is no trick to dust off now and then to lure an odd trout or two; many times it produces steadily when conventional dry-fly fishing fails, though it remained for a close friend—an expert fisherman—to open my eyes to its possibilities. By skipping and bouncing his fly he raised trout after trout throughout an entire afternoon, an afternoon when a free-floating fly failed to bring up a single fish.

Select a bushy, high-riding fly for skittering—a No.-10 bivisible works well—and use a leader point no finer than 2X. Cast directly across the current and allow the fly to swing on a perfectly taut line. Bring it through a cross-current arc in a series of short darts by pumping with the rod tip. Finish your retrieve, drop downstream a step or two, and cast again.

Skittering works best in broken, choppy water. The fly bounces along the top in a tantalizing manner and the rough surface reduces the leader's visibility. Strikes come with a wallop, so don't slug back on that tight line; you'll be surprised at how heavy a leader you can break by doing just that.

When you have worked a stretch with the skittering method, change to a smaller pattern and give the same water the conventional dry-fly treatment. Sometimes your skittering will stir them up to the point where they'll hit a free-floater.

Royal Coachman Fanwing

This is a recommendation based flatly on personal prejudice and proven to nobody's satisfaction but mine, so take it for whatever it may be worth. Long ago I gave up trying to match those evening hatches as a downright impossibility. By using a Royal Coachman Fanwing which imitates no known insect, I declare my colors in that respect and am relieved of one big worry.

Once I have tied it on, I leave it on until through fishing. Therefore I spend no time fretting whether this or that pattern wouldn't do better, and there goes worry number two.

I can see those big, white fanwings in the deepening dusk and this helps greatly in placing the fly over rising fish and in recognizing a strike.

Finally I generally wind up with a few of those twilight feeders in the creel; something I seldom did when I spent my time changing flies instead of fishing. Give the Royal Coachman Fanwing a try; stick with it through one of those fast and furious evening rises and see if it doesn't pay off.

Downstream

Upstream fishing is considered orthodox by the majority of dry-fly fishermen—a strong indication that downstreaming holds considerable merit.

Fishing a dry fly downstream you accomplish automatically what the upstreamer sometimes strives to do with little success—get the fly to the fish ahead of line and leader. Not only does the fly drift in advance of the leader, but it floats with less tendency to drag than when cast upstream. Then, too, strikes come on a fairly taut line and you hook more fish.

Stand at the head of a pool and cast a fairly long line downstream. Instead of letting your fly fall to the water at the end of the cast, yank it back toward you with the rod to

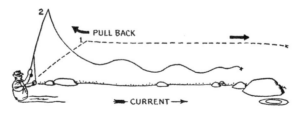

Downstream dry-fly cast without drag

drop it a short distance from you on a slack, wavy line. You'll get a dragless float until the slack is absorbed—plenty long enough to bring a rise.

Use the downstream method to fish broken water which would promptly drown a dry-fly cast from below. Drop your fly to the surface but hold the line above the water with a high-held rod. Let only fly and leader touch the water and you can get fish-taking floats where you thought them impossible.

Here's a downstreaming trick which takes fish found rising in stretches of glassy calm. Get well upstream from the rise and cast downstream to drop your fly far above the fish—far enough so he can't possibly see it fall. Now walk downstream at a pace to match the current and your fly will drift slowly and smoothly into his range of vision. A one-shot treatment, but one of the best for fooling trout in slow, smooth water. Use it in blind fishing, too. Make a single cast at the head of a smooth glide and walk your fly straight through. Much neater than repeated casting, which would only alarm trout in this type of water.

That Sinking Line

Don't despair when your line becomes waterlogged and persists in sinking. Fish out your float as usual, then draw the fly under with the sunken line and retrieve it slowly as a wet fly. The reason more trout aren't caught with a dry fly fished under the surface is because so few fishermen give it a chance.

Some dry-fly fishermen use a sinking line deliberately. Not only do they pick up bonus fish with the wet-fly retrieve, but they hold that by avoiding the surface disturbance of lifting a floating line, they put down fewer fish. Then, too, a sunken line assures a sunken leader—a whale of a help in dry-fly fishing but virtually impossible to achieve in smooth water by any other means.

Dapping and Bouncing

Dance a dry fly on the surface with line and leader in the air and no trout can resist it, provided that you are well hidden. Sneak up on those grass-hung pools of small meadow streams and dangle a bushy bivisible over the bank so that it just touches the water. Trout will leap to grab it if you've been stealthy in your approach. Work the same stunt over the sides of those plank bridges which always hide trout.

You can get the same effect by casting gently into overhanging foliage, on to a rock or atop a high bank and twitching your fly to drop it naturally on the water. Trout watch for insects to tumble into the stream from the banks and if you can fool them into thinking your fly fell by accident from a bush or clump of grass, you need go no further. Use a densely hackled bivisible which won't snag

WET FLIES AND NYMPHS

The time-honored method of fishing a wet fly consists of casting downstream and retrieving against the current with a jerking motion. You can take trout with this conventional technique but don't jump to the conclusion that it's the only way to fish a wet fly . . . or the best. Actually, you'll take more and bigger fish if you do an about-face.

Fish Upstream

Upstream wet-fly fishing soon separates the men from the boys. Cast to the head of a pool and your fly promptly sinks out of sight. Will a trout grab it if you give it no "action"? You bet he will!

Let your wet fly come back toward you with a dead drift. Nymphs and larvae have but limited swimming powers and tumble downstream at the whim of the current when dislodged from the bottom. Trout will mistake your drifting fly for just such items of food and test its edibility. Work it with the rod and you only kill the deception.

But with a sunken fly and a slack line, how can you sense a strike?

Watch Your Line!

Strip in the slack as fast as the current brings it to you, and watch your line for the slightest check or pause. Trout don't always hit a drifting wet fly vigorously, so set the hook when the line hesitates the least bit. It may be a log or stone, of course, but it *may* be a trout—a matter of speculation that makes upstream wet-fly fishing such a fascinating method.

Some will advise you to fish a greased line, and there is no question but what a floating line is easier to "read" for strikes. Others may tell you to go so far as to rig a big, bushy bivisible near the top of the leader and use this as a bobber. Makes strikes even more noticeable, all right, and you *may* take a fish now and then on the floating fly.

But I want neither a floating line nor a "bobber" for my wet-fly fishing. If your line floats, then generally your leader tends to do the same and the upshot of all this is to hold your fly so close to the surface that it does little good. I want my line to go down, dragging fly and leader after it—I'm playing for bottom feeders, and the deeper my fly goes, the better I like it. To detect strikes, I watch that point where the line sinks under the water.

Flashes

Almost always a trout will roll or "flash" when he takes your sunken fly and the merest suggestion of a glint or gleam should be a signal to strike quickly. Many, many times I have stuck at what seemed more an imaginary flicker than a real flash, only to feel the hook sink home in a fish. Seldom does your imagination play tricks on you in this respect; nine times out of ten the slight show of color that prompts you to strike instinctively is the flash of a deep-lying trout that has taken your fly—at least that's the way it works with me. The danger lies not in yielding to the impulse to hit promptly but in letting the opportunity pass.

Fishing a sunken line calls for cool nerves, razor-sharp reception, and a fine sense of timing if you are to hook fish. Nevertheless, fooling trout comes first; hooking them when they hit is something you figure out after you hit on the most productive method. This, in the case of upstream wet-fly fishing, is with a sunken line.

Fish Them Deep

Once again, fish the drifting wet fly as close to the bottom as you can get it. In quiet, deep pools you may need a split shot to help take your fly down. A weighted leader doesn't cast smoothly, but who counts any cast as too difficult if the fly winds up in a trout's jaw?

In water of average depth and less, a shot will have you hung on bottom too much of the time, so here it's better to depend on undertows and plunging currents to draw your fly down. You can usually sink your fly deep by casting well above each pool, directly into the fast water before it drops in. The current sucks the fly down as soon as it enters the pool and carries it along the bottom. If you cast into the pool itself, your fly will ride the upper levels ineffectively, so shoot it farther upstream to take advantage of the undertow.

Nymphs, Too

Upstream wet-fly fishing is nymph fishing. Use a true nymph pattern and you get right down to business by imitating the appearance of a nymph as well as its action. It can't help but improve your chances.

Probably you've noticed that wet flies frequently become increasingly effective when well chewed and stripped of some of their plumage. That's because they look more like nymphs than they did originally. You don't have to wait for wear and tear to effect this change. Trim a wet fly with a pair of scissors down to little more than the body and a few sprigs of hackle and wings and you have a good nymph pattern.

Fish a nymph upstream exactly as you would a wet fly—on a sunken line with a dead drift. You can fish a nymph downstream, of course, but don't give it the darting surface action used in downstream wet-fly fishing. Keep it as deep as possible and work it but slowly, if at all.

Nymphs in the Riffles

Here's a trick to try when you see trout "bulging" in the runs—swirling to take nymphs under the surface but boiling the water with backs and tails.

Pinch a sinker or large buckshot on the end of your leader and tie a six-inch dropper at about mid-length. Tie a small nymph on the dropper and cast to the middle of the run. Keep your rod high and line taut so the trailing nymph vibrates seductively just under the surface while the sinker holds against the bottom. Hold fast until you get a hit or the sinker lets go and lodges farther downstream.

Nymphs in Ponds

A tiny nymph or a small, well-trimmed wet fly often works on those hard-to-take pond trout. Try a very sparse pattern on a No.-14 hook and let fly and line sink to the bottom before you start your retrieve. Bring the fly in slowly with tiny hitches and be ready to set the hook instantly at the slightest tug. Avoid pronounced action; make the nymph creep along the bottom for best results.

Downstream Again

Whatever the superiority of upstream wet-fly fishing, the downstream method deserves more attention than we have given it to this point. It takes trout and therefore rates consideration.

Better to cast across and retrieve through an arc than to cast straight downstream and retrieve directly against the current. Lay your fly against the opposite bank or well out in large streams, and pump it back across in short, darting spurts. Cast directly across, retrieve, take a step downstream, and cast again; in this way you cover virtually all the water and miss no bets. Most strikes will come as solid whacks against a taut line and your percentage of hooked fish will run high.

Fishing downstream, you depend largely upon the action of your fly to bring them up, so try to give it the appearance of life and vigor. Speed it up, slow it down, halt it completely—the more erratic its behavior, the greater its attraction.

Speaking of fetching wet-fly action, Newfoundland salmon fishermen have long used a neat trick to bring salmon to their flies, and the stunt carries over to trout fishing. Here it is.

Riffling Fly

Tie your wet fly to the leader with a regular Turle knot and draw it tight. Next, pass a simple half-hitch over the eye of the hook and cinch it tightly just behind the head of the fly, drawing the hitch to the under side of the fly. Now your leader comes away from the shank of the hook at an angle which causes the fly to "riffle."

Leader-to-fly knot for "riffling" fly

Riffling consists of swinging your fly through an arc on the surface so that it leaves a tiny wake or riffle behind it. Cast across stream with a short line and retrieve by gradually raising the tip of your rod. Don't twitch or "pump"—draw the fly through its arc at a smooth pace to make it plane along the surface. This action—riding the top, yet cutting the water with a visible commotion—is as killing as it is unique. Don't fail to try it on sophisticated trout. They may think they've seen everything, but rig your fly to riffle and show them how wrong they are.

Under the Brush

Don't pass up stretches too overhung with brush to permit casting. You can fish many of these places with a wet fly by working it downstream in the current. Drop your fly to the water and waggle the tip of your rod to force out slack. Make the fly dart in one position for several seconds, let out a little more slack, and work it again when it has dropped downstream a few feet. Trout lying under such heavy cover get to see few artificial flies and develop little sales resistance. Once hooked, though, the brush gives them a decided advantage, so treat them gently.

Leaders

Upstream wet-fly fishing calls for long, fine leaders, so use the same lengths and tapers as you would for dry flies of comparable size. You'll also do well to use a tapered leader when fishing downstream, though you'll break off flies in many striking fish if you go finer than a 2X point. Fortunately, the moving fly seems to hold a trout's attention and makes him less leader-conscious, so an extremely fine leader point seldom proves necessary. Don't economize on length; play the percentages and use the longest leader you can cast well in any and all types of fly fishing.

Pattern and Size

Wet-fly patterns run into the hundreds, and all take fish. Some, nevertheless, seem to have unique virtues which make them particularly well qualified for certain jobs.

I have known old-timers who never fished anything but a wet fly, fished in no direction but downstream, and used nothing but a Gray Hackle. They stuck to the single pattern because it produced fish, its thick collar of hackle fluffs and springs, when retrieved upstream, a killing action which has stood generations of wet-fly fishermen in good stead. Hackled in another color the fly would give the same action, of course, but gray leads the field, with brown a close second.

Brook trout fall for bright, contrasting colors, and gaudy patterns like the Parmachene Belle, Silver Doctor, Royal Coachman, and Montreal have well-deserved reputations as brookie killers.

For upstream fishing choose a dull-colored pattern to match the drab shades of natural nymphs. The Quill Gordon, Cahill, and March Brown do this exceptionally well. A gloomy, but effective, creation of my own I tie as follows:

Wings: Sections from a matched pair of crow feathers.
Tail: Divided sections from the same feathers.
Body: Spun muskrat fur.
Hackle: Black.

Sparsely tied wet fly

Use small wet flies when fishing with a dead drift and turn to larger sizes when giving your fly action. Stock up with 12's and 14's for upstream wet-fly fishing, and include a few 16's, too. Sizes 8 and 10 are good bets for general downstream fishing, but don't hesitate to tie on a No. 6 where trout run to fairly large size. Bigger trout hesitate to chase after a moving fly unless assured of a mouthful.

Look for sparsely tied wet flies on hooks of heavy wire. Thin wings and scanty hackle have more trout appeal and are the tip-off to an expertly tied wet fly. Sparsely dressed on a heavy hook, a fly sinks down to where it looks right when it gets there.

Night Fishing

Have a few heavily dressed flies on No.-4 hooks, just in case you want to try a little night fishing. You can take big trout at night on bait, but you can also take them on flies.

Select a spot with ample room for a backcast and good water in front of you—and stay there. Big trout move at night, so let them come to you instead of wallowing around in the dark, hanging your fly repeatedly and wearing your temper thin.

Try to put your fly over any fish you hear feeding and keep your line as extended as possible, since you have no means of detecting slack.

Match that big fly with a heavy leader—a level strand of six-pound test—for visibility is not a factor in night fishing, and you'll horse back plenty hard when you hear a mighty Slosh that sounds like a five-pounder!

BUCKTAILS AND STREAMERS

A friend and I were once fishing a stream famous for its brook trout, but at a time when high water made fly fishing anything but easy. A white streamer finally turned the trick and I took six or eight good fish, though my friend failed to stir up so much as a strike with the identical pattern.

Puzzled, I watched him fish for several minutes and finally spotted the trouble.

Fall-back

Watch a minnow swim against a current, for minnow action is what you should try to give your streamers. The little fellow darts ahead in short spurts, but what happens when he stops his forward thrust: does he stay put until he decides to go ahead once more? Not on your life; the current yanks him back downstream until he forges forward again. Actually, he may not go anywhere; his forward spurts merely keep him in one relative position by precisely offsetting his back-drift.

Drawing a streamer or bucktail against the current with a steady, unfaltering progress, as my friend did, offers a poor imitation of minnow action. Match each series of forward darts with almost the same amount of fall-back, and you've achieved immeasurable improvement.

This technique holds the key to success in fishing all flies and lures which simulate minnows. It spelled the difference between success and failure for my friend, for he took fish as soon as he put a little "back-spin" on his streamer.

The Stand-still Retrieve

Minnows don't swim up and down a pool continuously, and your streamer or bucktail needn't in order to produce strikes. Here's a variation of the regular retrieve with which I have good luck and a way to tease those trout who can't quite make up their minds to slam full-tilt into a passing streamer.

Work your fly into a promising spot—off the point of a log or under an overhanging limb—and then make it dart ahead and fall back repeatedly in that one place, just as a minnow might do. Keep at it for several minutes; trout lying under the log or in the shadow of the branch will become increasingly itchy to make a pass at it, and frequently will if you tease them long enough.

Pattern

In bucktail and streamer fishing, choice of pattern seems less important than in any other type of fly fishing. No patterns look particularly minnowlike when motionless, but *all* of them have a realistic minnow action when fished properly. Action is the big thing. A simple pattern such as a plain brown and white bucktail produces as many strikes as a more elaborate creation when both are fished exactly the same.

Speaking of simple patterns, here's one you may like to try:

Wing: White marabou, with a single strand of peacock herl down each side.

Body: Silver tinsel.

I tie this pattern on a No.-12 hook, for marabou gives a small-minnow effect impossible to get with other materials. The thin, dark side-stripe conforms to the coloration of many tiny bait fish, and the horizontal line accentuates the fly's action. It's a killer on brook trout, but don't ask me why the brookies show special interest in it. Maybe it has just worked out that way for me.

Size

Big streamers and bucktails tied on No. 4's and 6's tempt the lunkers, but you'll miss a lot of good streamer fishing if you overlook the small sizes—tiny streamers and bucktails in sizes 10, 12, and 14.

Fish these small flies on a tapered leader and you'll take average-size trout who pass up big bucktails as just too big to tackle. You won't compromise, either, for the tiny streamers take big trout, too.

When to Fish Them

Trout take bucktails and streamers early in the season, and at other times when water levels and temperatures cause them to ignore all other flies. Use your bucktails for early and high-water fishing, but don't conclude that those are the only times when they take trout.

Once, when the water was low and clear, I worked a favorite pool to a fare-thee-well with small dry flies, but got not so much as a smell for my pains. Sure that the pool held trout, and, reluctant to give up, I tied on a small streamer and cast it to where my dry fly had recently floated. A pound-and-a-half brook trout rose to meet it with a spray-tossing Kerwhoosh and nailed it with reckless enthusiasm.

Carry a generous supply of bucktails and streamers in your book. They produce throughout the entire season—especially the small sizes—so don't hesitate to try them at any time in any type of water. If trout come as hard for you as they do for me, you can't afford to overlook a single bet.

Go Deep

Smaller trout will rise to belt a bucktail fished close to the surface, but the big fellows like to have them drop down where they live, though to get them there is sometimes easier said than done. Bucktails and streamers seldom prove effective when cast directly upstream and allowed to drift back, so it's not practical to depend upon descending currents to draw them under, as it is with wet flies and nymphs.

You can sink them fairly well down, however, by casting upstream and across. By the time the fly floats below you on a slack line it will have settled to a considerable depth, and this is the time to start your retrieve. Take advantage of every chance to sink your fly, for the deeper you get it the bigger fish it takes.

Weight does the trick, of course, but sometimes you need as much as a buckshot and this makes casting awkward and unpleasant. It helps, however, if you don't object to the sound of lead whizzing by your ear each time you cast.

Reeling in

I'd bet that more than once you've reeled up with an air of finality, determined to call it a day, only to get a smashing strike while reeling. That strike was no accident, for something about the action of a reeled fly often provokes strikes from trout who are buying nothing else. They seem to hit reeled bucktails and streamers most often and you may find it pays to use a "reel retrieve" as a deliberate technique.

Pick a long pool or run for the stunt and extend your fly beyond casting distance (unless you're a whizz of a caster) by letting the current carry out slack. Strip line right down to the backing and follow with some of that if the pool is long enough to take it. When your fly reaches the tail of the pool, start to reel at a steady, brisk pace, exactly as though you had decided to call it quits, and keep reeling until you either get a hit or bring the fly through the entire pool.

Work this trick every so often and you'll be pleasantly surprised at the trout you pick up.

Streamer and Dropper

To lend a convincing note of realism to your bucktail or streamer, try this trick: Tie a medium-sized to large streamer to your leader, then rig a dropper about two feet above it. To the dropper fasten a No.-14 wet fly or nymph. The idea is to give watching trout the impression that there goes a minnow chasing a fleeing insect of some sort. Have the streamer close behind the nymph and apparently on the verge of catching it, for this seems to make the hook-up especially convincing.

To work this trick you should forget about the fall-back action and zip the flies through the water to imitate an all-out chase. I get in my best licks with this trick in quiet water where I first can let the flies sink to the bottom and rest there a few moments. Then up from the bottom zooms the nymph with the "minnow" in hot pursuit. Small trout sometimes dart in to steal the nymph, but worth-while fish almost always go for the streamer.

Trolling

If you fish for trout in lakes and ponds, don't overlook buck-tails and streamers as effective and unique trolling lures. Not only do they take those heavy lake fish but they make it possible for you to troll with a fly rod—a sporting proposition in every sense of the word.

Rig up with an eight- or nine-foot level leader of about four-to six-pound test on an ungreased silk line that will sink quickly. Tie a streamer to the end of a leader and another as a dropper about four feet above it; flies trolled in tandem seem to hold the edge over a single streamer, and there *is* such a thing as scoring a double! Streamers on the large side do the best job, so use Nos. 4 and 6.

Let out 50 or 60 feet of line and make sure that it sinks. If it persists in laying out on the surface, hold the tip of your rod under the water until the line has sunk, for a floating line kills your chances. Troll along rocky shorelines and cover all known reefs, boulder-strewn shoals, and similar shallow, pocketed water.

If the wind blows up a chop, so much the better. Waves carry food—minnows, fry, and insects—close to shore and their pounding dislodges nymphs and larvae from the bottom. Trout move into the agitated water to feed, so head for the windy shore and troll close to it. The chop may toss you around a bit but it works wonders in making the trout hit.

Troll your streamers at a faster clip than you would a spoon, spinner, or sewn minnow, and give them additional appeal by constantly twitching the line through the guides or pumping the rod. Erratic action—sudden spurts and darts—brings strikes while trolling just as it does in stream fishing.

Let strikes come against no tension but the click of the reel. The spool's inertia sets the hook, and line pays out before anything can break, an important consideration when a rugged four-pounder lays into your fast-moving fly. Have plenty of backing under your fly line in case he decides to head for the other end of the lake.

OTHER FLY-ROD LURES

This chapter deals with fly fishing, but let's not overlook one of the most killing fly-rod lures known just because it's made of metal. Pure trout poison:

The Wobbling Spoon

Many of the metal wobblers are put out in tiny sizes for fly-rod use and heading the list is the familiar pattern striped with red and white. A mean, cussed thing to cast and an uncertain hooker, but does it bring up the trout!

Use a short, heavy leader—six-foot, six-pound test—for easier casting and work the lure downstream. With a little practice you can cover the water with a minimum of casting. Keep the spoon ahead of you, or to either side, by a continuous series of short roll casts and you seldom need to resort to a full-blown cast to put the lure where you want it.

Flutter and fall-back is the lethal prescription. Work the spoon as you would a streamer and it will stir up plenty of excitement. Many fish will show without striking, many more will strike without hooking, and you may finish without much sag on the creel strap, but you'll get action.

Trout frequently behave strangely in response to a fluttering spoon and you often need nerves of steel to set the hook in them. In the space of seconds a trout may make dozen zooming passes with such flashing speed that your eyes can't follow him. All this time you must keep the lure fluttering and darting to hold his attention, and resist the temptation to set the hook lest you yank the spoon away from him and put him down for good.

With these little red and white fly-rod wobblers I have, at one time or another, snagged a surprising variety of game fish—landlocked salmon, northern pike, walleyes, bass, trout, and down on through the ranks of yellow perch, crappies and other panfish. Nevertheless, I never think of these small spoons without recalling one particular trout. Not because of his size, although he was a sleek two-pound rainbow, but because he made such a sap out of me before I had the sweet satisfaction of finally cleaning his clock.

He lived under the tangled branches and roots of a flood-lodged tree in the crook of a deep, sharp bend. To reach his protected hideout it was necessary to cast from the bank, high above the stream. The wobbler seemed the best answer, for I could drop it in the stream below me, then work it with the help of the current until it fluttered its way beneath the sunken branches. I let it disappear into this retreat on a slack line, then worked it back out in a series of spurts.

It had no more than reappeared when the rainbow charged it, white mouth wide open. Zip, zip, zoom, zoom! He dashed at the spoon, ducked back, dashed out again so fast and so many times that it seemed that certainly he must be twins. Never once did he touch the lure, and to try to set the hook I knew to be rank folly. Nevertheless, each dart brought an urge to do so that was next to overpowering. Finally my nerves let go with a snap, and I gave a mighty yank as once more he dove in—and my rod broke like a wind-torn reed. Not that I hooked the fish; again he never so much as touched the spoon. My nervous yank, combined with the unusual angle at which I was fishing, had done the dirty work.

Fortunately, I had an extra tip in its case in the car. *Unfortunately*, it wasn't the tip that had broken. The middle joint had snapped cleanly at the base of the top ferrule. I hadn't felt so foolish since the time I hooked a dog on my backcast and smashed a treasured rod to smithereens.

I took stock of my resources; mainly a knife that featured not only a sharp blade but one of those pointed stilettos that comes in handy in plucking knots from leaders, punching holes in leather, and so on. It would do, I concluded.

Gathering a few twigs, I started a small fire and began the slow process of charring the section of bamboo that remained in the ferrule to a point where I could pick it loose with the stiletto. I removed it bit by bit, then managed to jab out the pin with the same tool. (Why must they pin ferrules!) Working carefully, I scraped the rod section to a new, snug fit, and at last pressed it home in the base of the ferrule. Lacking winding thread (as usual), I wrapped the serrated end of the ferrule with a length of leader material. Some three quarters of an hour later I was once more ready for his nibs.

I fully expected the battle of nerves to take up where it had left off, but in this I was pleasantly surprised. Instead of swooping and swirling at the wobbler as before, the trout tore out and belted it a healthy clout the instant it came within reach. There followed considerable ruction dangerously close to the matted roots and branches of the tree, but that particular trout was one baby I had no intentions of losing. Some minutes later I gave him the coup de grâce and carefully closed the creel cover on his silvery form.

Flatfish

Fish this little lure exactly as you do the wobblers. It has terrific action when worked, and dives down to fish-taking depths. On a slack line it floats, and this is a distinct help in working it downstream without casting. Hard to cast and a poor hooker like the wobbler, but it's in a class by itself as a big-trout lure. One of the best for trolling for big trout, landlocked salmon, and lakers.

3. Spinning

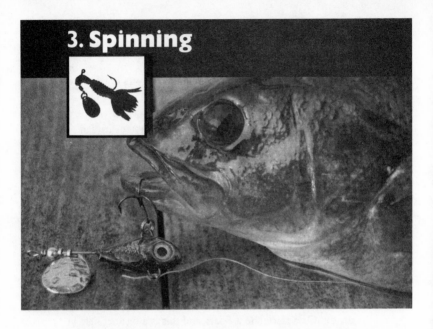

MOST OF US HAVE TO TAKE OUR FISHING WHERE
and when we find it, under whatever conditions prevail at
the time. My first crack at a certain Vermont stream came
at the end of a business trip which wound up in the vicinity
too early in the season for decent fishing. To make matters
worse, local spring rains had poured a flood of cold water
into the stream (a large one) and it ran bank-full and murky.
Nevertheless, I traded my evening meal for the chance to
fish during the few remaining hours of daylight.

Serious wading was out of the question, and the high,
cloudy water gave few hints as to where the trout might lie.
It was purely a case of chuck and chance it.

Dismal conditions to the contrary, I soon had a pound-size
rainbow in the creel, followed it with one of two pounds—I

am not making this up—and buried both under a thumping three-pounder, this one a brown.

The answer? Spinning! Let me dwell on this personal experience a little longer, because it summarizes so completely the remarkable virtues of spinning.

Distance

First of all, casting had to be done from the shore. A flick of the wrist sent my small spoon across the stream like a bullet and enabled me to rake the water with long, bank-to-bank strokes. Only a spinning rig could possibly cover such big water with a light trout lure.

Casting range, alone, accounted for the brown. Noticing the mouth of a small brook on the far side of the stream, I took aim and let fly with the spoon. Luck granted me a bull's-eye and the brown—probably attracted by the brook's clear flow—nailed the spoon savagely before it wobbled three feet.

Faced with identical demands and conditions, a fly rod would have been hopelessly inadequate. There was no room for backcasts and, had long casts been possible, flies would have undoubtedly been ignored in that cold, roily water.

Early Season Fishing

Some fly-fishing fanatics would rather catch nothing on feathers and fur than try some other method more in line with difficult water conditions. Most of us find little comfort in this particular brand of stone wall-butting. Spinning will take trout when flies won't, so turn to it in such times of trouble with a clear conscience. You can't afford to sneer at a method capable of taking six pounds of trout from cold, roily water.

Six pounds in three fish, mind you, which brings us to another charming characteristic of spin fishing.

You Take Bigger Trout

Lunkers have a taste for glittering hardware, and with a spinning rod you can feed it to them as never before. A fluttering spoon arouses heavy fish to a high state of excitement. Often they meet it with a furious, swirling attack as though they regard its intrusion as an impertinent challenge. In any event, you can depend on spinning gear to bring up trophy-size trout.

Spinning gives incredible range to your casting. It produces trout when fly fishing is all but useless. It takes those boosters which send you rushing to the nearest set of tested scales.

Spinning Lines

If your spin fishing doesn't call for extremely long casts, I would suggest a braided nylon line. It handles nicely and seems to take knots with less weakening than monofilament. For big-water fishing you need the long yards which a monofilament adds to your casting range. Don't forget to test all knots after you tie them.

Six-pound test casts well and is plenty strong for general fishing. You can handle large fish on lighter lines but the heavier weight will save you a small fortune in snagged lures over the course of a season. By dropping down to a finer line you add even more distance to your casts, but you can throw most lures a country mile with the six-pound line.

Spinning Lures

They'll have two kinds—trout and sucker; dozens of the former and hundreds of the latter. I know because I'm a Grade A sucker with a tackle box full of gadgets no sane trout would look at twice. I should drop them down a manhole but I value my collection as a monument to man's gullibility—mine, at least.

Beware of trashy spinning lures, for, in spinning, the lure you tie on seems to have more bearing upon your luck than in any other form of trout fishing. I took licking after licking with the creations which first hit the market, then started to score with heartening regularity as soon as I managed to find a few worth-while lures. I still try those early failures every once in a while, but they continue to come up with nothing.

In choosing your spinning lures, stick to the wobblers—short and broad, long and narrow—and pass up the true spinners which revolve on a shaft. You can take trout with some of the spinners, of course, but you can take more on the wobblers.

Teasing Action

Give them the same flutter and fall-back routine that you do the fly-rod lures and streamers. In slow currents cast across and downstream, dropping your lure as close to the opposite bank as possible to avoid frightening the fish with a midstream splash. Swing it away from the shore and retrieve slo-o-o-wly against the current. When you have the lure swimming straight upstream, stop reeling and pump several times with the rod, dropping the tip quickly after each pump to let the spoon flutter back on a slack line and regain depth. Pump a half-dozen times, reel a few turns, pump again; con-

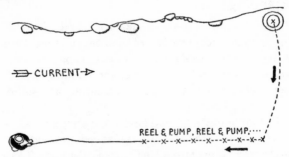

Fishing a spinning lure: reel and pump

tinue this faltering, erratic retrieve at the greatest possible depth and you'll hook three trout to every one you'll take by reeling steadily and rapidly.

Don't overlook the "stationary" retrieve as a trout-teasing trick in spinning. Bring the lure into a likely spot and let it hang there while you pump with the rod. Don't give it too much action—just a feeble flutter—and keep it tumbling for minutes at a time. Something big may zoom up and whale it when you have worn his resistance thin.

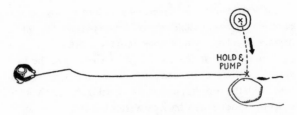

Fishing a spinning lure: hold and pump

Reverse English

But this is sometimes even more provocative: Make a short cast directly in front of you, start the pumping action, but follow each series of pumps with a few *backward* turns of the reel. Your wobbler darts forward and falls back as before, but its net progress is downstream instead of up. Consider, for a moment, the possible effect of this action on a fish lying downstream from you.

He first sees your lure as a distant flash. This arouses his interest but he's too crafty to come out of hiding and rip into it. The lure flashes again, but closer this time, for you have released a few turns of line; your trout watches with sharpened curiosity. Whatever the thing is, it seems unable to cope with the current; therefore, it must be crippled and harmless. Suddenly it dawns on him that if he just sits tight the struggling whatever-it-may-be will drift straight into his waiting jaws. Easy pickings! He poises to grab—just let that thing come a couple of feet closer. Wham!

Silly, of course, to assume that a fish reasons in any such complex manner, but the fact remains that a lure traveling upstream subjects a trout to but one fleeting moment of temptation: when it passes his hideout. If he resists a momentary impulse to dash out and grab it, your golden chance has gone. Not so with a lure which drops slowly

Fishing a spinning lure: pump and drop back

down toward him from upstream. From the moment he first glimpses it, his predatory instinct must withstand a steadily mounting temptation. No mere refusal to strike at first sight assures his safety; he must endure the lure's tantalizing approach and, finally, allow it to flutter by his very nose untouched. Some trout just haven't that much will power.

Aside from its teasing action, this "reverse" retrieve helps you to work your lure into the hard-to-reach spots which defy the most accurate casts. Let the current carry your spoon under thick, overhanging foliage and down into the depths of those sharp turns and bends where trout love to lurk.

You can work the same dodge on long, straight runs by simply walking the lure downstream. Cast well below you, pump your rod a few times, drop downstream a step, pump some more, step again. This puts fish on the platter if for no other reason than your lure works for you 100 percent of the time.

Depth

The deeper you can sink every trout lure but a dry fly, the more and larger trout you'll take. Aside from holding particular appeal for big trout, metal spinning lures are easy to fish at the lunker level. In moderate currents you can get your lure down where it belongs while fishing downstream. Retrieve slowly, allow frequent fall-back, and the weight of your metal spoon will keep it well sunk. Give it the reverse English treatment in spots where the current picks up, to compensate for the increased tendency to plane toward the top.

Fast, deep pools may tax your ability to fish a deep-running spoon unless you cast upstream. Then the lure sinks rapidly on a slack line in the fastest currents. Start your retrieve when you judge the spoon is close to the bottom, and try to keep it down there by slacking off with the reel frequently. Takes trout from those deep holes—also logs, brush, and old automobile tires if you miscalculate the depth.

Streamers Take Them, Too

You can buy bucktails and streamers tied on hooks weighted for spin casting, weight the hooks, and tie them yourself, or use a conventional streamer by pinching a buckshot on the leader about six inches ahead of the fly. The buckshot-fly combination seems to give more alluring action. The lead-bodied spinning streamer sinks like a stone when you relax the line as in a twitching retrieve, and this tendency to plummet toward bottom betrays it as an inanimate object to be avoided. When you use a buckshot ahead of your fly, it's the shot which sinks with a dead drop as soon as you slack off. The sinking shot tips the streamer and gives it the appearance of *diving* to a lower depth instead of sinking lifelessly. By alternately reeling and twitching you can give your streamer a lively dipping and rising action which is especially fetching in quiet water where the fly is particularly responsive to the tug of the shot.

Spinning gives you the chance to work bucktails and streamers at their most effective depths—something you can't do easily with a fly rod. I rate them several cuts beneath the metal spoons for day-to-day effectiveness but, nevertheless, my best spin-caught trout to date fell to a large streamer fished behind a buckshot.

Try Switch-hitting

Hand a man a spinning rod on Opening Day, permit him to fish with nothing else until the season closes, and he'll take his share of trout. Early and late, high water and low, spinning produces, but interlace it with fly fishing to get the greatest possible net gain. Happy to relate, spinning seems to produce best when fly fishing slumps to its worst, and vice versa. Ride the crest by switching from one to the other to meet prevailing conditions.

Don't let stubbornness cheat you out of good fishing as it did me, even after I had owned a spinning outfit for some time. When I went after trout with dry flies, I either took them with the floaters or just didn't take them at all. Finally I had sense enough to turn to spinning when the trout wouldn't look at my flies, and results sold me on the quick switch with the very first try.

It had been too rainy and cold for dry-fly fishing to start up, but hatches were long overdue, and besides, I *wanted* to take a few trout on dry flies. So I flogged the icy water of a half-mile stretch and, of course, raised not a single fish. Fortunately, I had brains enough to return to the car, break out the spinning rod, and give it a try. From the same section of stream a wobbling spoon soon produced four plump brook trout in the pound-or-better class. From that time on, I have rushed for the spinning rod whenever the weather steps in and puts a damper on fly fishing.

The spinning rod, itself, has a built-in feature of outstanding merit—it can double as a fly rod. Play this advantage to the hilt; carry two reels with you on the stream—a spinning reel and a fly reel—and use them interchangeably on the single rod. Hatches sometimes appear when least expected. Stand ready to switch from metal lures to dry flies when the trout suddenly start feeding on the surface. Or fish upstream with flies and explore the more attractive spots with a spoon on the way back.

You'll find that it often pays surprisingly well to cover water with both flies and spinning lures. You frequently take trout from a pool on floating flies on your way upstream, then snag a good fish with a spoon on your return trip. Then, too, you may see a heavy fish rising while fishing with a spinning lure. Trout feeding on insects seldom fall for a spoon so it pays to switch reels on the spot and offer him a dry fly. Something of a bother to change, sure, but who counts bother when it comes to taking a big trout? So tuck a fly reel in your jacket when you set out to spin fish.

Hooking

In spin fishing you won't have much to say about setting the hook. Either the trout hangs himself, or he's gone before you can do anything about it. In any event, you'll miss plenty of strikes when trout dart in, nip at your spoon, and escape without snagging. They seldom return, once they taste the metal.

Most strikes come against a taut line, which helps to hook any trout who makes a determined pass at your lure. Sometimes, when casting from a high bank, for example, the swirling attack of a trout takes place in plain view. This can be extremely upsetting, especially if the trout is a big one who makes several false passes at your spoon before hitting it. The natural inclination in such circumstances is to slow the retrieve to keep the lure over the fish as long as possible. Try not to yield to this impulse for, sure as anything, just as your lure loses all forward motion the fish will finally make up his mind to clip it. He hits on a slack line, the hooks fail to penetrate, and by the time you give that inevitable, desperate jerk, the trout has departed and your lure sails into the top of the least accessible tree. Things like that make you feel like smashing your rod over your knee and turning to knitting or raising geraniums.

When you see a fish make those hair-raising, zooming feints and swirls, try to maintain your normal rate of retrieve to make the hooks bite when the trout hits. If you must slack off, set to pumping rapidly. Then you have a 50-50 chance of jerking the lure just as the trout clamps it in his jaws.

Playing Fish

With a little practice the left-handed reeling which spinning requires will not seem awkward—perfectly natural, as a matter of fact. Once you master port-side reeling, you'll have no trouble handling big fish . . . if you have the drag set at the proper tension. Tend to this matter before setting out, for once you hook a fish, both hands will be busy (under no circumstances release that reel handle!) and to readjust drag tension while under fire poses a problem of considerable magnitude.

A few encounters with heavy trout will demonstrate the importance of drag adjustment. Set it too soft, and the fish goes zinging off with yards and yards of line which, unless you're lucky, he'll have snubbed around something before you can recoup. Too much drag usually results in disaster before you have time to do anything about it.

A drag which yields to a swimming fish may prove too harsh if he somersaults and hits the spool with the sudden acceleration which he gains by cartwheeling aloft. I learned this to my sorrow when a big rainbow made a wild, soaring leap and, through some law of physics known only to himself, straightened the hook against a line of six-pound test.

Since then I have leaned toward a light drag adjustment. If a heavy, sharp jerk against a lure hanging in a strong current turns the spool a few clicks, I'm satisfied that I have the drag set where I want it.

In setting your drag tension, remember that by stripping line from the spool you don't get a true indication of the force needed to pull line through the guides. The surge of a fighting fish comes at right angles to the plane of the spool, and considerable resulting friction is added to whatever drag you supply. Test total braking effect by hooking your lure under a root, or elsewhere, and flexing the rod against it. Make sure that the spool yields to a sudden jerk.

Netting Fish

This normally simple process is somewhat complicated in spinning and can cause embarrassment the first few times you try it. If you release the reel handle you can't hold your fish and, obviously, you must retain your grip on the rod. Where's the third hand coming from to use the net? Trig the line by pressing the lip of the spool with your right forefinger and you can let go the reel handle and wield the net with your left hand. Switch the rod to the other hand if you'd rather net with the right.

Spinning with Bait

Not only has spinning, with its glittering metal lures and revolutionary method of casting, blazed a new trout-fishing trail; it lends added range and finesse to the time-tested tricks of bait fishing. Use your spinning tackle to bait-fish large streams and you can cover water which you could never reach with a fly rod.

Sewn Minnow

The most killing of all big-trout baits, the average-size minnow places a severe strain on a fly rod and permits casts of only moderate distance, always a serious handicap in river fishing for trout. Those across-stream spots of promise—eddies and backwaters, projecting boulders and fallen trees—you must pass up with exasperating frequency simply because they are out of range of a fly rod.

Rig a sewn minnow on your spinning outfit and all sense of overbalance and excessive weight disappears instantly. A light cast whips your minnow out an incredible distance and you suddenly realize that spinning is the answer to a minnow fisherman's prayer.

Cast upstream and across, let your bait drift to a point opposite or below you, then bring it in with a slow, erratic retrieve. Notice that the fine line offers minimum resistance to the current and lets your minnow sink quickly each time you slack off. Use this gained advantage to sound out and probe those deep retreats where the big minnow-feeders hide out during the day.

If your minnow needs the flash of a spinner to attract trout in roily or cold water, the additional weight of the necessary hardware only adds to your casting range. The same goes for a buckshot if you pinch one on to get down to the lowest levels of extremely deep holes.

Spinning Bobber

Minnows cast well on a spinning rod because of their natural weight. You can handle all other baits, even the tiniest and lightest, with the help of these tiny plastic bobbers or "bubbles" made especially for spinning. These little floats have plugs to admit varying amounts of water to give the desired casting weight. You can cast a large nightcrawler, for instance, with little or no water in the float, but to cast a natural nymph on a tiny hook you'll need to fill the bobber nearly full.

Attach your bobber about four feet above the hook—it won't cast well if you go higher—and fish upstream. The bobber carries the bait back at the exact speed of the current, so you get a drift with practically no drag. Not only can you drift your bait far out in a large stream, but the bobber prevents the constant snagging which invariably results when you cast bait upstream with a fly rod.

With the spinning rod and bobber you can work the rivers with all those tiny baits that take trout. There's hardly an end to bait possibilities, but here's a suggestion for low, clear water:

Tie three feet of 3X nylon below the bobber and rig it with a No.-14 hook and a single split shot. Bait the hook with one or two caddis worms and fish upstream through fast, shallow runs. The nearly filled bobber rides low in the water where the slightest tug will draw it under. Calls for sharp eyes and strict attention to business, but trout lying in

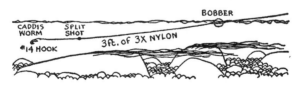

Upstream nymph rig

the riffles snap up those drifting larvae when they'll hardly look at anything else.

Substitute a wet fly or artificial nymph for the caddis worms and you fish these two lures the way they should be fished for greatest effectiveness—upstream and back with a dead drift. Grease your trigger finger, though, for you have to hit fast when that bobber dips!

Strip Baits

Cut one of those wriggling belly strips from a trout and you have another first-class spinning bait. Cast it as is, or add a buckshot to give more distance. Shoot it across-stream and retrieve against the current to give it that killing swimming action. Play the same tune with the tail half of a large minnow. These baits may turn the trick on big trout when whole minnows fail.

Lakes, Too

Bet you know of at least one lake or pond where trout grow big, but where you can't get to first base with a fly rod. Try spinning to fool some of those fish who won't give your flies a tumble. Go after them early in the season when they're close to the top. Comb the water along the shore with your favorite spoons and see if you don't start taking fish.

Use your spinning rod for trolling, too. Those little spinning lures are just as deadly when trolled as when cast, and they make a light tackle game of trolling. Troll at low speed and keep your rod twitching to give the lure additional action. Make sure to set the drag lightly enough to pay out line with a strike.

When warming water sends the trout to lower levels, you can still get your spinning lures to them. Make long casts while anchored or drifting slowly, and let your spoon sink almost to the bottom before you start it in. Reel slowly, with frequent halts, to keep your lure in the cooler depths which hold the trout.

Tough customers, those lake fish, but many of them meet their match in the spinning outfit.

Tricks that take trout? Well, let's put it this way: Tricks that take *some* trout. Trout would hardly merit the elaborate processes evolved for their capture if they yielded easily. Use the best tackle money can buy, cram your skull to the bursting point with "know-how," and you'll be lucky to fool one trout in ten—one in 50 probably comes closer to the truth! This doesn't necessarily prove that trout are smarter than you, though your neighbors will surely toy with that inference. Should they make the claim openly, you can point out that you haven't yet been caught by a trout. You must admit, however, that this distinction hardly gives you the right to take yourself overseriously on the streams. Some make that mistake and miss most of the fun of trout fishing. Deadly serious and unbending, they take their lickings with poor grace, and few people can suppress a snicker when they come home, as they frequently do, with long faces and empty creels.

Fish for fun! Consider yourself lucky when you score, and shrug off defeat as something you had coming to you. Learn to relax and roll with the punches. You'll wind up with a heavier creel and be a far better man to have around the house.

4. Bait Fishing for Bass

SOMETIME, SOMEWHERE, THE FISHERMEN OF THIS country should erect a national monument in honor of the black bass. Probably they should build two—one for the smallmouth, and another for his cousin, the largemouth. East and west, north and south, the two species thrive in uncounted lakes, ponds, and streams. True aristocrats among fresh-water game fish, they live in almost everybody's backyard where they stand ready to take on all comers, no holds barred and no quarter asked or given.

Thanks to a bucking two-pound smallmouth, I came to know the feel of a leaping, plunging fish at the age of six. What game fish but a bass would have grabbed the worm which dangled from my cane pole, and what but the mighty, gill-rattling leap which instantly followed would have left a six-year-old so thrilled and bug-eyed? I can still see the bronze bombshell which exploded before my startled eyes, and feel the powerful surge which doubled my pole and all but tore it from my grasp. This I knew, instantly and for all time, was something a man could live for.

Bass not only live everywhere; they eat almost everything and anything. Consequently, you can take them on a wide variety of baits, though you won't find them pushovers for your natural offerings. Now and then you'll strike a day when they come to a certain bait—nightcrawlers, for example— like puppies to a feed pan, but these days come few and far apart. To take bass day in and day out on bait calls for skill, knowledge, and trickery, which is true for any worth-while fish.

Where to Look for Them

You can't take bass if you don't know where they are, so the first trick in bass fishing is knowing where to find them.

Where you look depends upon which kind of bass you're after, smallmouths or largemouths. The two species have individual preferences with regard to water temperature, depth, bottom characteristics, and cover which you should take into consideration when looking for one or the other. In general, look for largemouths in comparatively warm, shallow water along the shores. They like weed beds, coves, patches of lily pads, shoreline pockets, and the shade of overhanging foliage. They lurk under driftwood, and a sub-merged tree or brush heap almost always caters to a full house. Given suitable cover—shade, weeds, pads, or jutting logs—they take up positions within a few feet of shore in water no deeper than a couple of feet or so. Sunlight and warming water may drive them offshore during the middle of the day, but they move back in the evening and stay until the sun gets high the next day.

Typical habitat of largemouth black bass

Smallmouths like cooler, deeper water over rocky, boulder-strewn bottoms. Look for them along the edges of sharp drop-offs where they can cruise briefly in the shallower level for bait fish, then drop back into the depths to cool off. Sunken reefs often have bass along their edges, and the fish lie along the sides of stony points which continue underwater. Where the bottom falls away abruptly from shore, smallmouths generally lurk close by, waiting for small fish and frogs to make the fatal mistake of venturing too far afield. You'll find them along the faces of cliffs and ledges where large sections of rock have fallen to make underwater caves and retreats.

You can run down the largemouth hot spots by watching for visible clues to their location. Shoreline stumps indicate sunken trees, coves lead to areas protected by shade, and you can detect weed beds with little trouble. Finding the

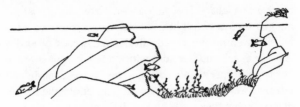

Typical habitat of smallmouth black bass

spots favored by smallmouths may not prove so easy. These may lie a considerable distance from shore with no tip-offs to help you discover them. Here a sounding weight comes in handy for probing the bottom and leading you to good bass grounds.

Let's say you know of a shallow bay with a weedy bottom—good breeding grounds for perch and other small fish—and you suspect smallmouths of raiding this supply of food. In the evening they come into the bay to feed, but where do they hang out during the day? Start at the mouth of the bay and work toward the open lake, taking soundings every few feet. Depth may increase only slightly for some distance, then drop suddenly to a much lower level. Return to the shelf, anchor close to the lip of the drop-off, and fish over the edge in the deep water. Don't forget that a few feet can make all the difference in the world. More than once I've anchored where my partner in the stern hooked bass after bass while I couldn't get a nibble fishing from the bow.

Reefs are tough to locate, for they may rise up anywhere in a lake. Sometimes they stand above the surface during periods of extremely low water, or they may lie so close to the top that waves break over them when the wind stirs up a heavy chop. Ordinarily, though, you locate these hallowed grounds purely by accident, if at all. Certainly you won't learn about them from other bass fishermen, though you can bet that each hidden reef is well known to at least a few.

Once you find a glory hole far removed from shore, make certain before leaving that you can come back again with reasonable accuracy. Pick out a landmark on shore, imagine a line running from it through the boat to the opposite side of the lake, and tie it in with an object on that side. Do the same with another pair of points whose connecting line

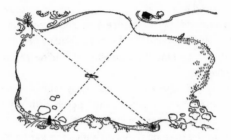

How to fix the location of a hidden shoal by cross bearings

runs roughly at right angles with the first. To return to the same spot, simply cruise along one of the imaginary lines until you cross the other; you should miss by no more than a few yards at the most. Better jot those landmarks down on paper, though; you can't afford to trust such an important matter to memory alone.

Just as it pays to differentiate between largemouths and smallmouths when seeking their feeding grounds, it behooves you to cater to the individual tastes of the two species in the matter of baits. Anything which works on one will work on the other, but not always with the same degree of success. In general, largemouths fall for big baits while the smallmouths find bite-size morsels more tempting. Just as you would suspect from his oversize mouth and rounded paunch, the largemouth finds it hard to resist a six-inch chub or a big green frog—baits which offer complete meals. The trimmer smallmouth, on the other hand, likes tidbits—hellgrammites, for example—which his cousin sometimes scorns as too tiny to merit consideration. Of course, plenty of smallmouths tangle with big baits, and vice versa; just remember that the percentages are in favor of the general rule.

Hooks, Leaders, and Sinkers

Bass, compared to trout, for instance, are not particularly shy fish. They'll rip into almost anything, as a matter of fact, if they happen to feel in a fighting mood. But don't let their comparative lack of fear lead you into the mistake made so frequently by bass fishermen—that of overlooking the importance of small hooks, light leaders, and tiny sinkers. Bass may not flee for their lives at the slightest disturbance, but don't think for a moment that they lack shrewdness. For every one you catch on heavy, crude tackle, there are dozens you *won't* fool until you switch to lighter gear.

You don't need a big hook to land a bass; a No. 6 does the job just as well as a 6/0. In addition, the No. 6 gives greater freedom to your live bait than does a heavy hook, permits it to live longer, and doesn't detract nearly as seriously from its natural appearance. Many a bass has taken a minnow on a large hook, only to reject it instantly when he senses that he was a mixed mouthful of steel and minnow. A small hook not only brings more strikes, but it encourages more bass to hold the bait once they have taken it.

Most bass fishermen wouldn't dream of using a hook as small as a No. 6 for bass but it can double the number of strikes. Try it with all but the largest baits and see for yourself. You don't need a much bigger hook for large minnows, either; a No. 4 is as far as you need to go. Drop down to a No. 8, too, when you use small, tender baits such as crickets and grasshoppers. Small hooks, big bass!

Match your small hooks with light leaders and watch the production rate zoom upward. When fishing in deep water free from obstructions, a leader of three-pound test gives you all the strength you need to lick the biggest bass, and helps mightily to hook just such a cagey customer in clear water. Weed-loaded shallows give fish a chance to get a direct pull on the leader so here you must use a heavier weight. A leader which tests six pounds proves adequate in most instances, although ten pounds is safer when you hook a monster largemouth amid weeds or snags.

Important step number three: Go easy on sinkers! Many bass baits require no additional weight to sink in the quiet waters of ponds and lakes, and they produce many more strikes when fished with no sinker at all. Toss these baits out on a light leader, let them settle slowly and naturally, and bass frequently gather them in before they reach bottom—something they seldom do with a bait dragged down rapidly by a heavy weight. Larger, livelier baits such as minnows and frogs actually need but little sinker weight to drop them down to the bottom levels. Just pinch a couple of split shot on your leader and watch how it affects your minnow. He fights the drag of the small sinkers successfully for a few moments, then tires and the weight drags him down a foot or so before he resumes his efforts. Instead of plummeting downward, he fights a slow, losing battle with the two split shot and his gradual, struggling descent has almost irresistible bass appeal. Not only that, the tiny shot do not have the suspicious appearance of a heavy chunk of lead and don't drag against the fish alarmingly once he takes your bait.

Small hooks, light leaders, and little or no sinker: three big steps toward catching more bass. Unless you're a rare exception, you've fished for bass up to now with much heavier terminal tackle than you actually need for the job. No harm done? Those big hooks, coarse leaders, and heavy sinkers rob you of bass after bass. Scale down the size of your gear and see for yourself!

Bobbers?

Yes and no. In shallow-water fishing you can use a bobber to good advantage in keeping your bait away from the boat and out of the weeds. Use a light float to put as little drag as possible on a bass once he takes the bait. Don't use one unless it serves some purpose, though. In deep water you have better control over your line if you use no bobber. Besides, a float adjusted for a depth greater than the length of your rod prevents you from reeling in enough line to land fish.

In choppy water a bobber keeps your bait dancing and the constant motion helps to attract bass. In addition, the wind carries the float along slowly if you pay out slack and this gives you the chance to cover a good deal of water from an anchored boat. Snap a bobber to your line whenever a favorable wind lets you send your bait drifting along the shore or over likely spots.

Baits for Bass

Bass eat just about anything they can swallow and some even choke to death trying to down fish, sometimes their own kind, which are just too big for their gullets. Hardly any living creature small enough to be swallowed can venture safely into bass water or hover above it. Bass make short work of mice foolish enough to go for a swim, and leap to snatch sparrows and blackbirds from bending reeds or drooping branches. Insects, worms, fish, salamanders, ducklings, crawfish, as well as a host of other creatures go down the same hatch if they don't watch out.

In the face of his completely democratic tastes and appetites the bass shows surprising restraint when you go after him with bait. Tempt him with this, tease him with that, and he may have none of either. Try a third item on him—sometimes the one you judge the least promising—and he may go for it as though starving. More often it takes more than three different offerings to discover the favored item of the moment, so carry the widest possible variety of baits when you go bass fishing.

The Worm

Make sure that your collection includes this universal standby. You may try earthworms—nightcrawlers and the smaller variety—six days running and get skunked completely. Then, just as you have about decided that bass never take worms, you suddenly hit the jackpot with them.

To fish worms for all they're worth, don't just let them hang, once you have them near bottom. Hook them lightly—a single crawler or three or four small worms—and cast gently to keep them on the hook. Allow them to settle slowly—I *hope* you've resisted the impulse to clamp on a sinker—and when they reach bottom let them lie there for a few moments. Now, draw them up two or three feet and let them sink back on a slack line. Do this a half-dozen times and, if nothing happens, retrieve them and cast again, this time at a different angle to hit new water. If you merely dangle your bait, bass must cruise close before they discover it. Recast frequently, raise and lower your bait between casts, and the action calls them from a distance.

When fishing in water on the shallow side, try this worming technique: Use a nightcrawler and hook it once through the head (the darker end). Cast as far from the boat as you can without losing your bait, and let the crawler sink to the bottom. If nothing picks it up after a short wait, start it back again along the bottom with the slowest retrieve you can manage; make it *crawl,* literally. Twist in but an inch or two of line at a time and pause between hitches for the worm—it should be a fresh and lively one—to do some crawling and squirming of its own.

Try this, too, when a single nightcrawler fails to ring the bell: Change to a larger hook, and hang on as many as five or six crawlers. Makes a tremendous gob, but how those worms squirm and writhe if lightly hooked! Keep this big wad of bait bobbing gently just off the bottom to get the last squirm from each worm. The oversize bait sometimes proves too great a temptation for bass to resist.

Sometimes a spinner and nightcrawler make a killing combination. Try casting a June-bug blade ahead of a single, head-hooked crawler and retrieve slowly and haltingly. Make the spinner flash, let the bait settle, then start it up again. Troll the same rig slowly or let it trail behind the boat as you drift. Draw it ahead with the rod frequently to make certain the spinner revolves.

Finally, keep your worms fresh and lively if you hope to get results with them. A wooden box keeps them cooler than does a metal can. Put your box under a boat seat where the sun can't get at it. On hot days, cover the box with wet burlap or other cloth; it prevents drying, and condensation keeps the worms cool.

Minnows

Here's another proven producer—the minnow—so carry a well-stocked bait bucket on every bass fishing trip. All kinds of minnows work well on bass, but the list by no means stops with the various minnow species. Small fallfish three to six inches long invariably make superb bass bait. Change their water frequently or hang them over the side as they seem to require more oxygen than most bait fish. Tiny perch, the smaller the better, belong on the preferred list, though bass fishermen frequently overlook them. In addition to attracting bass, these tough little chaps seldom expire before bass grab them. Small bullheads make even tougher bass bait and work well if you snip off their spines before using. Suckers rank close to the top and they, too, have the ability to stand the confinement of the minnow bucket and live for long periods on the hook. Sunfish the size of a half-dollar take bass, but seemingly not quite so well as the others.

Among the minnows, the common shiner and the "golden" or "pond" shiner may hold a slight edge over their more drab relatives, though all species come through with flying colors. If you have trouble getting minnows, settle gladly for any you can get and ask no questions. You can be sure that all take bass.

Hooking the Minnow

When still-fishing in ponds and lakes, hook your minnow lightly, just ahead of, or under, the dorsal fin. Slide the barb under the skin and out to avoid injuring the bait. Lob it out gently and drop it to the water as lightly as possible. The livelier your minnow, the more strikes you get, so take pains to keep your bait fresh and vigorous.

In moving water, or when you intend to "work" your minnow in any way, hook it through both lips. Hooked in this

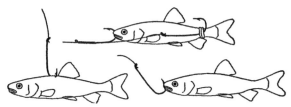

Three methods of hooking live minnows

manner your bait stays alive for a long time but, of course, tears from the hook easily if seized toward the tail. Take exceptional care to feed slack line with the strike when you fish with lip-hooked minnows.

When still-fishing with minnows from an anchored boat, it pays, just as it does with all baits, to raise and lower your minnow frequently to call the bass in. You don't have to recast your minnow; just draw him to the top and let him sink back on a loose line. If he struggles against no more than a split shot or two, he sinks slowly and his vain efforts to resist the slight but steady drag advertise him as easy pickings. Stir him up often while he is near bottom, too, to keep him off balance and struggling.

Still-fishing at anchor works fine when you know your bass grounds. If, in strange water, you make the unfortunate mistake of anchoring an eighth of a mile from the nearest bass, you're in for a fairly dull afternoon if you decide to wait them out. Unless you've taken bass there before, don't stay in one spot for more than ten minutes or so if it produces nothing. Instead, raise the anchor a few feet off bottom, drift about 100 feet, and drop it once more. Keep on the move until you find fish. Incidentally, this type of probing often turns up those hidden hot spots—channels, reefs, and bars—which have no visible clues to their location. Make sure to line them up so you can return, for you'll probably find bass there each time.

A trailed minnow sometimes works wonders in deep water, too, but here of course you need the weight of a sinker to take your bait down near the bottom. For this type of fishing it's wise to rig two hooks in tandem to increase your chances of hooking striking fish. Tie a No.-4 hook to the end of your leader and whip a No. 6 to the strand about a couple of inches higher. Run the smaller hook through both lips of the bait and secure the trailing hook back toward the minnow's tail by means of a tiny rubber band. Troll very slowly; try to give inspecting bass the impression that the minnow travels under his own power. Halt frequently to let the bait do some swimming on its own and to give the bass plenty of time to make up their minds.

If a slow pace produces nothing, rig a small spinner ahead of your bait and try stepping up your speed a notch or two. Lacking a spinner, kill the minnow and sew it on a hook so it spins slowly. Remember the sewing process: down through both lips with the hook, then down through the head, under the skin and out again near the tail, and draw the leader tight enough to produce the desired degree of curve. Even if you *do* have a spinner, sew on a minnow just the same and work the two in combination. Sometimes it takes all the flash and action you can supply to fetch a strike. Don't forget to use swivels with all spinning baits.

Setting the Hook

This is supposed to be a cut and dried business—the bass grabs your minnow, makes a run for it while you feed slack line, stops to swallow the bait, and you sock it to him when he moves off again. If you can find bass obliging enough to conform to this convenient behavior pattern, you shouldn't have much trouble hooking them. I haven't been that lucky. No two bass act alike with *my* minnows, and after 30 years of bass fishing I still yank and hope for the best.

I have a sneaking suspicion that when fishing with all but the largest minnows, you'll hook more bass by laying into them the instant they seize your bait! You hit on a short, tight line, the bass hasn't had time to reject the minnow, and generally has it completely enclosed in his mouth. Fine in theory to give a bass time to swallow the bait, but you also give him time to feel the prick of the barb, saw the line through weeds, feel the drag of any sinker and become suspicious for one of a dozen other reasons. One hint that the cards are stacked and he spits out your minnow and goes on his way. If you have trouble with the run-stop-swallow-run routine, try taking your chances in those first few seconds. Bet you miss fewer bass than you think you will.

Not so good though, to hair-trigger them when using a 6-inch minnow. Too often bass grab these big baits in positions which leave the hook outside their mouths. Better let them run and hope for the best. Have plenty of loose line stripped and coiled in the bottom of the boat and start stripping more as soon as a bass moves off with the minnow, lest a sudden spurt bring him against the reel and cause him to drop the bait. He'll probably stop before taking too much line and, you hope, swallow the minnow. Here again, you may only invite trouble by waiting until he moves off, for when he does he may leave the bait behind him. Better to give him time—a minute is plenty—to swallow the bait, tighten the line against him, and set the hook while you know he's still on. You won't connect every time, but you'll score more frequently than if you wait longer. Besides, nothing is more disappointing than to fiddle around for ten minutes or more and then have the bass leave before you even make your bid. Better to miss them hard and clean.

Frogs

Both species of bass like frogs, but you'll probably have better luck with tiny frogs for smallmouths and bigger ones for largemouths. The little, spotted leopard frogs make fine bait for smallmouths while the big, green fellows make the kind of a meal largemouths go for.

In general, you can fish frogs effectively by using the same tactics you employ with minnows. Still-fish them just above the bottom, trail them behind a slow-moving boat—on the surface near shore and weighted in deep water—or let them swim at the top over weeds or around pad patches. Hook frogs through both lips and they live until taken.

Hook a small, dead frog securely through the lips and you have an excellent skittering bait for bass (and pickerel, too). Cast it into the weeds or lily pads and bring it back with a series of jerks. Don't try to set the hook when you get a strike as the bass seldom has the hook in his mouth; give him a chance to engulf the entire bait first.

Sometimes you can lay your frog smack on a lily pad. Whenever you do this, let him rest there for several moments while you twitch the line very lightly to stir the supporting pad and create the impression that it holds a live frog. When you finally jerk the frog into the water a bass may be waiting with open mouth.

Tadpoles

You seldom see these little chaps in a bass fisherman's bait bucket, but put them in yours whenever you can get any. Best are the fat two-year-olds with bodies as big around as bottle caps. Hook tadpoles through the base of the tail and use no sinker, for they head for bottom of their own accord. They live almost indefinitely on the hook and wiggle constantly if you hold them just above the bottom. Give them an occasional twitch to keep them moving.

Live-bait dealers seldom offer tadpoles for sale and probably for that reason few fishermen use them. Let this be your cue to go to the nearest frog pond with a dip net and stock up with these fellows, for they make one of the finest deep-water bass baits. Use them in heavily fished waters to lure bass that shun the more conventional baits.

Hellgrammites

The dobson larva (hellgrammite) has won a well-deserved reputation as a bass bait, especially among those who go after smallmouths. Fished near the bottom, the hellgrammite frequently produces strikes when smallmouths will have nothing to do with any and all other baits.

Evil of appearance and mean of temperament—he'll give your finger a painful nip if you give him a chance—the hellgrammite has few attractive features save the hard shell which grows just back of his head. Grasp this shell between thumb and forefinger and slide the barb under it and out. Hooked under the collar he remains lively for a long time and won't tear loose if you handle him with reasonable care.

Hellgrammites work best when fished near bottom, but they crawl under rocks at the first opportunity. Once hidden, they anchor themselves firmly with a pair of tiny hooks which grow near the tail and you'll only succeed in tearing the hook free if you try to pull them loose. Snip those hooks off with a pair of scissors before fishing and you'll save a good many baits.

Use a leader at least six feet long of about three-pound test with a No.-8 hook. Weight the hellgrammite with a couple of split shot, let the line sink until the shot touches bottom, then take in just enough line to raise the bait clear. Jiggle the bait and recast frequently to attract the attention of all bass in the vicinity.

Once a bass takes your bait he'll swallow it at a single gulp, so don't hesitate to set the hook at the first sign of a strike. By hitting at once you hook the majority of bass in the jaw, allowing them to give a much better account of themselves than when hooked far back in the throat.

Very often you have difficulty obtaining hellgrammites from bait dealers, so it's wise to lay in a supply even if it means sacrificing time you could spend fishing. Dobson larvae live under rocks in the riffles of warm-water streams and can be caught by "screening." Frame a two-foot square of window screening, press it against the bottom on the downstream side of a rock, turn the rock over, and the current washes the dislodged insects against the screen where you can pick them off. You can speed up production greatly by enlisting the help of a fishing partner. Let him stir up the bottom and overturn stones with a stout hoe or rake while you hold the screen.

Hellgrammites have tough constitutions to match their appearance, so you can keep your supply alive for months. Place them in a tight wooden box, fill it with rotted wood, fix a screen over the top and store in a cool, dark place such as a dirt cellar. Keep the rotted wood slightly moist by sprinkling it sparingly with water from time to time, but don't let it become wet. Use a small wooden box for carrying hellgrammites on fishing trips and keep it in the shade as much as possible. Keep the box covered with a wet cloth on hot days as you do your supply of worms.

Crawfish

You have but to examine the stomachs of the bass you take to find conclusive proof that crawfish are a standard item of bass food. Both largemouths and smallmouths hold them in high esteem and give them more than passing attention to a hook baited with a live crawdad.

Crawfish, like hellgrammites, work best when fished just above the bottom with little or no sinker to hamper their natural movements. They also resemble dobson larvae in their efforts to hide under stones and crawl into crevices, so keep them raised a few inches above the bottom and move them often to make sure they remain visible to the fish.

Hook them through the tail and bring the barb clear to avoid missing strikes. Give bass time to get them in their mouths before you set the hook. Crawfish have pincers akin to those of the lobster, and bass swallow them only after working them into a position where they can't ply their nippers.

Each time a crawfish grows too large for his shell he sheds it to grow a bigger one. Though he makes haste to replace his cast-off armor, he must weather a period when he is in the soft-shell stage and doubly attractive to bass. Use soft-shelled crawfish whenever you can get them, but remember that bass love them hard or soft.

Look for crawfish under stones and waterlogged sticks along the shores of lakes and in the shallows of streams. You can grab them in your hand if you do it quickly, but a small dip net makes an easier job of it. Remember that the crawfish swims backward; hold the net behind him, threaten him with your hand, and he'll scuttle straight into the mesh. If you don't need them in a hurry, you can bait a trap with meat or fish, leave it overnight, and have crawdads galore, come morning.

Keep crawfish in a minnow bucket and see that they get plenty of fresh water. You want them alive and full of pep when you let them down for the bass to look over.

Crickets

Under ordinary circumstances, bass must see mighty few crickets in the course of a summer, and certainly never enough to make up a significant portion of their regular diet. Nevertheless, they seem to have a taste for these fat insects, and smallmouths, especially, fall for them hard and often. Try a single cricket on a small hook to tempt finicky feeders and if that doesn't work, thread six or eight on a larger hook as a king-size attraction. You'll find it impossible to keep crickets alive on the hook for any length of time, but don't let it bother you. Bass like them dead or alive, and by piercing them with the hook you may let out the very juices which make them so attractive. A friend of mine has a Brittany pup who delights in pointing crickets, so they may smell good for all we know.

Crickets are too tender to stay on the hook long, so stock up abundantly before setting out, to have plenty for re-baiting. Catch them under boards and flat stones early in the morning before the dew has left the grass.

Grasshoppers

Fish grasshoppers exactly as you do crickets and you'll get equally good results. Like crickets, grasshoppers soon die when placed on a hook, but lack of life makes little difference when you fish them under the surface.

But bass like to have hoppers served alive and kicking on the top of the water, too, and there's a way of doing that. Make a hopper harness by tying two short lengths of thread to the shank of a long-shank, light-wire hook. Bind a live grasshopper to the hook with the thread, cast him gently, and let him kick up a commotion. A fussy job, but bass come to expect occasional wind-borne hoppers and put a sudden end to any which come to their attention. Use the largest grasshoppers you can get; they are much easier to tie to the hook and their lustier kicking stirs up more fuss on the water.

Do your grasshopper hunting early in the morning or late in the evening. Cool air makes the hoppers lethargic and they're much easier to catch than during the heat of the day. Keep an eye peeled for those big locusts, too. Fish one of these fellows while his wings flail the water and you can expect results in a hurry if bass are around.

Grasshopper rig

The Early Bird

Almost every bass fisherman knows that the best fishing hours come early in the morning and in the evening. Many get to fish during twilight hours, but how many have the steely determination to crawl out of the covers early enough to fish at the misty break of day? Rugged medicine for most of us, but how the bass bite in those magic minutes when the first hint of daylight shows in the east!

Not enough to rise at dawn. You must be up and about in pitch darkness, row to your bass grounds before the first glimmer of light shows, and be anchored and fishing before you can make out objects on shore. Time it right and you won't have long to wait before things break wide open.

You owe it to yourself to sample some of that fast and furious dawn fishing. It takes raw courage to rise at two in the morning, but you'll find it well worth the suffering.

Less Noise, Please!

Probably bass couldn't hear you if you yelled your head off, but don't forget that they are keenly sensitive to vibrations transmitted directly to the water. Thump the gunwale with oar or paddle, scrape your tackle box along the bottom of the boat, or knock ashes from your pipe on the side and you warn every bass in the vicinity. Take care to preserve underwater silence by handling tackle box and minnow bucket without banging them against the boat and stow oars or paddles where they won't shift and roll. It's a good idea to wear sneakers or soft-soled shoes to avoid a constant scraping of feet. Some expert bass fishermen attach enough importance to the noise factor to lay a strip of old carpet material in the bottom of the boat to muffle the sounds of unavoidable movements.

Important, too, to observe silence and stealth while making your approach to a fishing spot. Cut the motor or ship the oars and drift into position whenever possible, instead of churning forward under a full head of steam. Go easy with the anchor. Lower it slowly on a tight rope; don't let it plunge down and thud to the bottom as though dropped from the sky. Shift about as little as possible while baiting up and lower your bait without fuss or splash. Many times a bass will grab your bait the instant it sinks down to his level . . . if you've taken care to come up on him quietly.

River Fishing

So far, we have treated bass fighing as strictly a pond and lake proposition, but bass also live in streams. Largemouth rivers are generally so sluggish that you can fish them exactly as you would a lake. Smallmouths, on the other hand, sometimes inhabit fast-moving, rocky streams where you can put your trout-fishing experience to good use. Quite often smallmouths share a stream with trout, and in such places it is common to catch one species while fishing for the other.

River smallmouths fall for all the baits which take their cousins in ponds and lakes, but the smaller baits handle with greater ease in moving water and you'll probably have your best luck with them. A lively nightcrawler makes a hard-to-beat river bait, though a drifted hellgrammite may deserve an even higher rating. Small minnows take plenty of river bass, too. Lip-hook them so you can handle them in the current and keep them alive at the same time. Try spinners ahead of minnows and worms when they produce no strikes by themselves.

Use only light sinkers—a couple of split shot—and depend upon the currents to drift your bait into likely places. Fish such baits as worms, nymphs, grasshoppers, and crickets on a slack line to prevent drag. While bass are not as shy as trout, they become suspicious if your bait behaves queerly so try to drift it as naturally as possible. Cast upstream and across and let the bait drift back toward you.

Look for bass in streams as you would for trout. Expect to find them wherever cover occurs close to major currents which they can watch for food. Bass seem to prowl about more than trout, so you'll also find them in quiet back-waters, dead-water coves, and shoreline shallows where trout seldom venture during daylight hours. They like pockets and caverns in ledges and lurk behind projecting tongues of rock.

Smallmouths never lack fighting ability wherever you find them but those living in streams head the list. Trimmer than lake bass and current-toughened, they give you a rousing fight on light tackle. Though on the average they run to smaller size in streams, you'll tangle with occasional lunkers. Set the hook in a four-pound river smallmouth, and he'll take your mind off your troubles for quite a few minutes!

Spinning

The spinning outfit and the small, spinning bobber make an ideal combination under many conditions. In shallow water along shore or in weedy bays, you can cover wide expanses from an anchored boat by simply making long casts at varying angles. Hook on a lively minnow, attach your bobber three feet above the hook, and cast as far as you can toss the minnow easily. Let the float rest where it lands for several minutes, then bring it closer to the boat with a few turns of the reel. Start it up again if nothing happens, and continue with alternate rests and short retrieves until you have brought the minnow to the boat. Cast again at a different angle to reach new water. Fish such baits as frogs, crawfish, and nightcrawlers in the same manner. Try a large minnow with no sinker or bobber. Cast the minnow close to bass cover and let it swim at the surface.

In deep water, try a nightcrawler or hellgrammite with a buckshot pinched to the line for casting weight. Lay out a long cast, let the bait sink, then bring it along the bottom by barely turning the reel handle. Retrieve only an inch or two at a time and pause between turns. The slightest motion attracts fish and few bass can resist snatching at a slow-moving bait.

In river fishing you'll find the spinning rod a great help in hitting all the promising spots with the small baits which work so well on smallmouths. Fill your plastic spinning bobber nearly full of water—it will still float—and you can make long casts with a nightcrawler or hellgrammite. Shoot your bait upstream and let it float back. You'll get a long, natural drift and no hungry smallmouth will pass up your offering. If trout are present, you'll tangle with them, too!

When it comes to fishing with live minnows, spinning ranks head and shoulders above any other method. You can drop your minnow into all the pockets, reach likely spots close to the opposite bank, and cover broad pools which you could never fish thoroughly with minnows on a fly rod. You can make even longer casts by switching to a sewn minnow and spinner combination, for then you can handle the bait as roughly as you please.

In short, spinning fills the bill whenever you need to get distance in your bait fishing. With the help of the water-weighted bobber you can make reasonably long casts with the smallest baits, while those heavy baits which overtax a fly rod you can heave into the next county. Fishing fine-and-far-off swings the odds in your favor, so make spinning play a regular role in your bass fishing.

Try Everything

How does any bass survive long enough to gain respectable size under present-day fishing pressure? Many do, you can be sure; probably far more than you suspect. Every one of these large bass has learned to fear and avoid conventional baits and lures; either that, or he inherited such caution. In either event, results are the same—he hasn't yet fallen for the fisherman's old routine, and he has no intention of doing so in the future.

What better trick than to offer these sophisticated lunkers something which they seldom see on a hook? Tadpoles belong in this category of off-trail baits as we have seen, but what about a wriggling salamander, for instance? Or a June bug? Or the meat from a fresh-water clam . . . a big snail, shell and all . . . a turtle the size of a half-dollar . . . a tiny snake! Bass eat all these and many more with perfect safety, for these creatures invariably show up minus hooks. Use one as bait and you have a good chance of catching the big fellows off balance.

Sometimes you can throw them off stride by pulling a switch with conventional baits—serving them up with a change of pace. Ever hook two minnows side by side on a single hook? It sometimes turns the trick when a lone minnow goes untouched. Bass seldom see a frog or crawfish trolled behind a spinner, which may be all the more reason for trying it. Eccentric behavior of a bait may spur bass into striking, so don't hesitate to stray from the beaten path when ordinary methods fail.

Summing Up

Learn where to look for bass: Shorelines, weed beds, and protected shallows for largemouths; reefs, rocky points, sharp drop-offs, and bars for smallmouths. Watch the shore for signs of largemouth hot spots; sound the bottom for sharp irregularities in depth which mean smallmouth holes. Look for both species closer to shore in the evening and early morning.

Use small hooks, fine leaders no shorter than six feet, and little or no sinker!

Carry a wide variety of baits. In general, offer large baits to largemouths, smaller morsels to smallmouths. Move all baits frequently to attract bass. Jig them often and recast from time to time.

Go looking for bass instead of waiting for them to come to you. Fish in one spot ten minutes, then drift on to a new location if nothing happens. Keep at it until you find fish. Avoid banging things against the boat and setting up underwater vibrations. Approach your fishing spots quietly and stir around as little as possible while fishing.

Try the unorthodox. When you can, use baits which bass seldom see on a hook. Fish conventional baits in manners that break with tradition when other methods fail.

Remember that the choice bass fishing hours come at each end of the day—dawn and dusk. You may get more action during the first hour of daylight and an hour at dusk than over the rest of the entire day. Fish early and late whenever possible, and lay off during the midday hours.

5. Plugs, Bugs, and Hardware

BASS MAY IGNORE YOUR MINNOWS, NIGHTCRAWL-
ers, and frogs—all legitimate items of food—then smash a
plug which looks like something out of a bad dream. Bass
plug designers seem to have outdone themselves in producing weird creations, yet they must know what they're
doing, for their most outlandish contraptions take fish.
What's more, plug casting for bass unquestionably ranks as
the country's most popular form of fishing.

Though you probably can catch as many bass on bait as on
plugs, plug casting gives you more for your money in terms
of sport. Pockets, partly submerged trees, and other targets
challenge your casting skill and accuracy, you keep your lure
moving almost constantly, and strikes come as sudden, solid
whacks against the rod.

Surface Lures

Absolutely tops for bait casting thrills! The plug floats where you can see it, striking bass raise a visible and audible commotion, and hooked fish really take to the air in the shallow water along shore where floating plugs work best.

Do your shoreline plugging in the late afternoon or early morning when bass lie in the shallow water. Use a floating plug which kicks up a commotion on the water when retrieved—the Arbogast Jitterbug and Heddon Crazy Crawler are two of the best—and *tease* those bass into striking.

Cast your floater out, then let it lie! Sometimes a bass will rise up and sock it as it lies motionless, but more often he'll keep within striking distance, hoping for an attempt at escape which will give him the excuse to charge. Play the game his way. Let your plug rest until the last ripple has died away or longer, then give it a sudden twitch. The bass will have been waiting for this very movement, your long wait will have made him increasingly impatient, and he'll streak for the "escaping" plug with all the speed he can muster.

Of course, your plug won't attract a bass every time it lands, but it may during the course of the retrieve if you work it all the way to the boat with alternate rests and provocative tremors and spurts. Then, too, some bass may have sufficient will power to refrain from striking at the first movement but will cast caution to the winds when you have regained all but a few feet of line. Make that plug dance, dip, and dart—always after resting it—and fish out every cast completely. Whang those hooks into a striking fish, too, for bass don't always hook themselves on a motionless or slowly moving surface plug.

Action sells the surface plug, but only if you chuck it where the bass lie. In shallow water bass like protecting cover, so pick your spots accordingly. Fish the edges of dense weed beds, drop your lure into patches of open water among lily pads, and whenever you find a sunken tree with a few gaunt limbs sticking above the surface, work it for all you have in you. Be daring in your casting. Lay your plug close against logs, shoot it into brushy tangles and as far under overhanging bushes as you can manage. Makes a much more interesting game of casting, and pays off in bass when you hit those difficult targets.

Remember, also, that the surface lures work best on a calm, glassy surface, so pick the lee shore whenever you have a breeze to contend with. At times when wind is no factor, choose the shoreline which casts a shadow in preference to one which faces the sun. The water cools earlier along the shaded bank and bass also seek the protection which the shadows afford.

Surface lures are constructed to stir up a fuss on the water, but you can add a feature to the best of them which sometimes helps to tease up strikes. Hang a short tail of pork rind on the trailing hooks, large enough to wiggle visibly, but not bulky enough to cut down the plug's built-in action. Instead of the rind, you can use a strip of thin rubber cut from a white balloon. Taper it to a point and fold the wide end before hooking to prevent it from tearing free. A strip of white belly skin from a fish or frog makes an equally effective substitute.

COLOR

Are bass color-blind? Not by a long shot, no matter what you may have heard. Tests have proven conclusively that bass are keenly discriminative when it comes to colors, and can distinguish between closely related shades.

Is the color of your lure important? Probably, when it comes to underwater plugs, but it's doubtful if color has much bearing on the success of a surface lure. They come in all colors, of course, but notice that the underside of every last one of them is white, and this is the only part of a floating plug that bass get a look at. Wouldn't a darker color be more conspicuous? Probably, but don't conclude that bass ignore your lures, whatever their color, because they fail to see them. It's a bass's business to see things in and on the water and he isn't going to overlook anything as large as a plug, even if it's virtually colorless. Moreover, practically all water creatures have white bellies and a surface plug with a white underside probably looks more lifelike to the bass. Above all, they work, so again we must admit that plug makers probably know their business better than we do.

Fish the Weeds, Too

Plenty of bass lie under those heavy, impenetrable mats of weeds, but how to get at them? Cast a plug into the tangle and it hangs up before you move it more than a few inches.

What you need here is something which skims along the top, and nothing serves this purpose better than the time-honored pork chunk. This lure consists of a chunk of salt pork with the tough rind left on, cut to any shape which strikes your fancy. Trim it to imitate a frog or settle for just a plain wedge-shape—it will take bass in any form.

Pork chunk lure. Note weed guard

Make your chunks of the proper weight for casting and you'll arrive at the appropriate size. Better toughen the chunks up before using by soaking them in formaldehyde for a week or so.

You'll need a 4/0 weedless hook to fish this lure and you should punch the barb through the tough rind at the "head" of the chunk. Cast it smack into the densest weed jungle, but don't let it sink! Hold your rod high and start reeling the instant the chunk hits the water or weed. The idea is to make it plane over the weeds, so hold as much of your line in the air as possible to get an upward pull on the chunk.

Bass may never get more than a fleeting glimpse of your skimming pork chunk, but this frequently works to your advantage. They know that something is skipping across their roof, and from its lively pace they judge it to be full of life and vigor. Such things need catching, so they rise up and nail it without bothering to make the close inspection which they would in open water.

Not but what the chunk works in open expanses. Use it anywhere you would tie on a surface plug, for it's a fine shallow-water lure under any circumstances. You may want to add a little color to its rather pasty appearance when you use it in the open, and you can do that by threading a few bits of red yarn through the fat with a needle. Does it

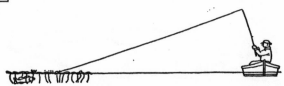

Method of fishing pork-chunk lure

help? Remember all things help in fishing if you *think* they do. The toughest man to beat is the one who has absolute confidence in his lure, for he refuses to take a licking.

If you don't want to bother with the preparation of pork chunks—be warned that it's worth your while!—you can turn to ready-made weedless lures, for the manufacturers have answers for everything. The No.-3 model Arbogast Hawaiian Wiggler, with weed guard and rubber skirt, brings up bass from the weed patches. Retrieve it as you do your pork chunk—with a high line—and the lure skims along on its back with the hook riding free in the air. Additional effective weedless lures include the other Arbogast surface-runners, the Heddon Queen, True Temper Dixie Wiggler, Johnson Silver Minnow with weed guard and pork rind, and the R-Jay Brook's No.-4.

The biggest thrills in bass plugging may come with shore-line fishing, but you can't count on finding bass close to shore in the middle of bright, hot days. They move out into deeper, cooler water and you must either follow them out or run the risk of going fishless.

Diving Lures

As you move offshore you'd better forget your surface plugs and put your faith in plugs of this type. They float on the surface while left at rest—a welcome feature while you pluck at a backlash—but dive under and wiggle enticingly when retrieved. Though action comes built into these lures, you can display it to best advantage if you use variety and change of pace in manipulating them, instead of merely casting and reeling in.

Cast and let your plug lie on the surface a few moments as when using a floating lure. If nothing happens, twitch it sharply to make it pop under in a sudden dive, but slack off immediately to let it return to the top. If this fails to stir up a strike, draw the plug under, begin your retrieve, but vary the speed. Reel rapidly to draw the plug down, slow down, pump with the rod, speed up again—remember that you aren't playing on hunger alone. Make your plug appear elusive and hard to catch, and a bass with stomach crammed may take a sporting swipe at it.

If you have trouble provoking strikes, tie a tail of red yarn to the rear hooks of your plug, or a fluttering strip of balloon rubber as you did with your surface lures. Stirs up action many times, but take care to use a thin, light strip which won't slow down your plug's wiggle.

Sinking Lures

Bass sometimes go to surprising depths, either in search of food or to find cover and comfortable water temperatures. Lake trout fishermen sometimes hook bass while trolling at depths of 60 or more feet, and they probably venture even lower than that at times.

At any rate, much good bass fishing goes to waste simply because fishermen don't take the trouble to get lures down to where the fish have congregated. Any bait fisherman can tell you that bass often lie in 20 feet of water or more. These fish take minnows, frogs, crawfish, and other bait in their deep retreats, and they'll hit your plugs, too, if you sink them down where the fish can see them.

Even though these lures, and many other good ones, sink of their own weight, you won't keep them down near the bottom by simply casting and reeling. Make your cast, let the lure sink close to the bottom before starting it in, then move it at an extremely slow pace to keep it at the greatest possible depth.

The secret of deep-water bass fishing lies in observing these two rules, so they bear repeating: Let the lure sink before retrieving, then move it so slowly that it wobbles just off the bottom. Simple though these two rules sound, you may have difficulty in heeding them. If you don't watch your step, you'll become impatient with waiting after each cast for your lure to sink and, after a few tries, conclude that a retrieve so slow gives your plug insufficient action to attract fish. Try to remember that you *can't* retrieve too slowly. Just a hint of action will bring strikes from bass in deep water. Just as important, only a slow retrieve keeps your lure down where the bass are. Take a few slow turns of the reel, twitch the rod once or twice, let the lure settle, then take a few more turns. This sounds like dull work only *before* you have seen how it takes bass. Dredge a few lunkers from the depths and you'll make those slow, deadly retrieves with the keenest anticipation.

Actually, it's tougher to locate deep-water bass than it is to catch them once you find them. A sounding weight comes in as handy here as it does in bait fishing, so use it to locate sunken channels, reefs, bars, and sharp drop-offs. With the casting rod, however, you can cover far more water from a fixed point than while bait fishing, so this simplifies the problem somewhat.

Let's say that you have dropped anchor in a spot where you hope to find bass. By fanning your casts out from the boat like the spokes of a wheel you can cover more than a half-acre of water before moving on. Do just that; lay out casts on all sides of the boat, bring the lure slowly along the bottom, and move to a new location only if you complete the circle without a strike. With average luck you'll run into bass before long and you generally can take several whenever you locate favored grounds.

If there is next to no breeze, let the boat drift until you find fish. Lower the anchor the moment you get a hit, though, for you'll want to give the surrounding water a thorough workout. Don't try drifting when any appreciable wind is blowing, for invariably you'll move too fast to work your lure at the lowest depths. Much better to anchor, work a spot, drift on, and anchor again.

On the other hand, maybe you won't need to do much exploring. Perhaps you know the deep-eater bass grounds of your favorite lakes but have concluded that you could take fish from the deep holes only with bait. Not so. Give them a look at a slow-moving, deep-running plug, and see if they don't take hold!

Those Small Lures

Oversize bass plugs which hark back to bait casting's earliest days are rapidly giving way to smaller lures, either new creations or scaled-down versions of the old favorites. For reasons known only to themselves, bass took those big plugs, and still do, but in heavily fished water it becomes more and more of a job to take a string of bass on the jumbo-sized lures.

Just how bass come to fear and respect baits which fooled their ancestors on a wholesale scale remains a mystery. Obviously, few of them can learn by experience, for a single mistake generally has fatal consequences. Nevertheless, learn they do, as indeed they must to survive. Bear this in mind before concluding that nearby lakes have become fished out.

If your old reliables have yielded fewer and fewer returns, it doesn't necessarily mean that the bass population is on the wane. Before giving up, swith to something new and different in the smallest size you can cast. Try fishing with greater care, too. Make long casts, especially when fishing shallow water, avoid thumping the boat, and approach likely spots slowly and quietly. Make each cast count instead of flailing away mechanically. Analyze your techniques and methods for possible flaws and make refinements, no matter how slight, wherever you find need for them. The improvement may appear insignificant at first glance but may give you a new lease on life in hard-fished waters.

Try a Minnow

Most of us have forgotten that bait casting originally meant what the term implies, and that the free-spooling reel and short, stiff rod were developed to cast one of the most productive bass baits known—the minnow.

The still fisherman with his minnow bucket is a common sight on all bass lakes, but how many bait casters you see using a dead minnow as a lure? To be more specific, when did you last cast a minnow with your bait-casting outfit?

Here you have a casting lure so outdated that it ranks as a novelty in almost any bass water, and novelty is what gives you the edge over sophisticated bass. What's more, a minnow represents real food, and don't think for a moment that bass, as well as other fish, can't tell the difference. With a plug you must fool bass with action alone, but they know a minnow is edible before they grab it.

So sew a five-inch minnow—a tough-skinned sucker or chub—securely to a snelled hook and give it just enough curve to produce a slow roll with your retrieve. Use it with no sinker along shore and fish it somewhat as you do your surface plugs. Make its motion more continued, however, as you're offering a meal now, instead of teasing bass with challenging action. Make the bait appear to swim, but erratically enough to give the impression that it's injured and having a hard time of it.

Use the same bait in deep water by pinching a sinker a foot ahead of the hook. Let the minnow sink to the bottom, then bring it in with slow turns of the reel. In either case, along shore or in deep water, you can set the hook immediately or wait for the bass to swallow the minnow. My choice is to hit him instantly as I would if using a plug.

Didn't granddad cast frogs, too? Say, you're catching on fast!

FLY FISHING

The popularity of bait casting notwithstanding, many fishermen refuse to class any form of fishing as tops which doesn't involve the use of the fly rod. In fairness to the fly-casting enthusiasts it must be admitted that no other casting instrument yet devised has the supple grace and balance of the fly rod, and through no other method can the fisherman experience anything which compares with the pleasant sensation of fly casting. Then too, the pliant fly rod makes the most of the scrap once a fish is hooked. You have but to feel a four-ounce rod come to life under the rushes of a sizable fish to realize the truth of this statement.

Fortunately, you don't have to shelve your fly rod when you turn to bass fishing. One of the most respected characteristics of both smallmouths and largemouths is their willingness to tangle with almost anything, and they respond to fly-rod offerings with gratifying enthusiasm.

Bucktail and Streamers

Old-fashioned bass flies offered neither tantalizing action nor imitation of any known form of bass food. Bucktails and streamers do both. In action and appearance they resemble small-bait fish. Bass go for them in a big way.

We've already mentioned that bass have a keen sense of color and that the color scheme of an underwater lure probably helps to determine its success. This seems to hold true with bucktails and streamers, for the gayer patterns win highest favor among both bass and fishermen. You'll find that it pays to use a fly which features red in some way, with yellow ranking as another preferred shade. The Mickey Finn which combines these two colors is one of the best bass flies you can use. The common red and white bucktail makes another killing lure, as does a white marabou streamer with a slash of red at the throat.

Fly fishing for bass is, of course, shallow-water business and practical only during the hours when bass hug the shoreline. Cast to the likely covers and pockets with your bucktail or streamer just as you do with surface plugs. Pause after casting a streamer as you do with top-water lures. This gives bass a chance to eye your fly and also lets it settle beneath the surface where it best resembles a minnow. After a brief wait—sooner than with a floating plug—start the fly back toward the boat with a slow, jerky retrieve. Make the streamer dart forward several times, halt it and allow it to sink as though helpless, then snap it forward with marked briskness. A sudden show of life when least expected makes many a bass rush in for the kill in spite of his better judgment.

If you tie your own flies you can turn out a pattern which combines the effectiveness of a floating lure with that of the sunken streamer or bucktail. To a No.-4 streamer hook, tie a tail of bucktail as heavy as you would use for the "wings" of a conventional bucktail pattern. Now wind the shank of the hook with hackle as you would a bivisible. Use this creation with an undressed line—you want the line to sink when casting bucktails and streamers—and let it lie motionless on the surface after you cast. Give it a few slight twitches, then pull it under with the sunken line and complete your retrieve as if using an ordinary streamer pattern. The floating-sinking pattern produces strikes on the surface and fools bass when retrieved to imitate a minnow. Gives you a chance to offer the bass a choice of action with each cast.

As soon as you tie a spinner ahead of your fly you make casting a chore . . . but you take more bass. Not only does the glittering spinner serve as an attracter, but it helps to take your fly down where it does the most good. Use your favorite streamer pattern as is, then precede it with a small spinner and see if it doesn't become even more effective.

Don't overlook the possibilities of the spinner-fly combination for fishing water of considerable depth. Cast, let the lure sink close to the bottom, then retrieve in the usual manner. Deep-lurking bass will hit a streamer as readily as those near shore if you give them the chance.

Spinners don't work well ahead of flies tied on hooks with either turned-down or turned-up eyes, so use straight ringed-eye hooks if you tie your own. Then you can add that helpful hardware whenever you need it.

You can drop down to small hook sizes and take small-mouths. In fact, a No. 8 or 10 on a long, fine leader may fool them when they shy away from larger flies. Trout fishermen will tell you they take bass on 12's and 14's when fishing for trout in water inhabited by both species. In general, and especially for largemouths, it's best to offer something bulkier, however. Patterns tied on No.-4 hooks work well for general bass fishing, though you can sometimes tempt more largemouths with a bigger size. Big marabou streamers look like satisfying mouthfuls and you have hard work to beat them as largemouth flies.

The Calcasieu Pig Boat

In Maplewood, Louisiana, my good friend Tom Nixon lives, fishes, and ties flies; the latter of such quality and design as to bring comfort and joy to local anglers, calamity and distress to all bass and panfish within the sphere of their influence. Most famed of his bass flies is an original—the Calcasieu Pig Boat—but before I say more of that, or pass on some of his fishing and fly-tying tips, let me tell you the wonderfully pleasant way in which I first came to know Tom himself.

Some time along in last December I had very good reason to become seriously worried. My supply of lemon wood-duck side feathers had dwindled to the point where I could see very plainly that I was going to run short of ammunition come trout season. Many Quill Gordons, Hendricksons, and the like remained to be tied and none of the all-important wood-duck plumage to tie them from. Then one morning a small package arrived. It contained dozens and dozens of the beautiful and sorely needed feathers. It was from Tom with a note asking if I could use them.

We have swapped flies and traded many letters, however, and the products of both his fly-tying vise and his pen have the unmistakable qualities that mark the true sportsman, craftsman, and fellow who knows his fishing. The following insight is his, and for which my indebtedness to him grows even greater.

Calcasieu Pig Boat: "Strictly a bass fly." (So says Tom, but I have plans for fooling both him and some big old brown by dropping it some dark night where I think the latter will be cruising around.) "No. 4 hook; black chenille body palmered with long, black hackle; abundant shoulder hackle of strands of state-gray rubber about once-and-a-half as long as the hook; black head with eyes painted red in fields of yellow;

A "Calcasieu Pig Boat" bass fly

weed guard of wire." (It would look like a bass-killer to me even though I didn't have Tom's word for it.)

"The weed guard plays an important part in fishing this fly, for I cast it four or five feet up on the bank, let it lie a full minute or so" . . . (the mark of a real fish-trickster!) . . . "then flip it into the water as though it had jumped from shore on its own. The weed guard prevents the fly from hanging up, and the same goes for around cypress roots and tangled marsh grass."

Weed Guards: "The best material I have found for making weed guards is the wire used for control lines on model planes, size .010 inches or .008 inches. It comes on cardboard holders about six inches in diameter, which means that it is loosely looped and doesn't have to be straightened before using.

"For a guard, cut a strand of wire which, when doubled back on itself, will reach from the head of the fly to slightly beyond the bend of the hook. Crimp the two strands about a quarter-inch ahead of the bend and bind this flattened section into the head of the fly on the underside of the shank. The two wires now extend back toward the point of the hook at a fairly sharp angle from the shank; to make them more efficient, crimp each strand, about three eighths of an inch from the end, bending the wire so the end section runs nearly parallel to the barb of the hook, but about a half-inch below it. The point is now guarded by a springy wire on either side. The wire will give with a strike, but will let the fly slide through glass and branches without snagging."

The Woolly Worm: "I like to tie Woolly Worms on hooks with bent shanks such as Herter's English Bait Hooks. I think the fly looks more like a true caterpillar, for the bent body gives the idea of motion—humping or coiling in true caterpillar style. The fly seems to hook as well, if not better, than when tied on straight-shank hooks." (I have one of his Woolly Worms, and it sure looks convincing. Bent-shank hooks for me, too, when it comes to Woolly Worms in the future.)

All-around lure: "A Black Gnat tied palmer works well around here for bream, and sometimes bass, but the same Black Gnat becomes a better all-around lure if you add a small pork rind and run a nickel spinner ahead of it. On this combination I have taken not only bass and bream, but even catfish."

Fishing the Wind: "Along the low, marshy Gulf Coast of Louisiana the flow of the rivers is affected by the wind. These tidal rivers are very deep, slow moving, and, for the most part, bordered by marshes and swamps. A strong south wind blows water from the gulf into the rivers, impeding, or even reversing, the flow for as far inland as 60 miles. This raises the level of the water, whereas a strong north wind had the opposite effect, dropping the water a full 18 inches, or even more.

"A south wind and rising water usually means good fishing, but when fishing during a blow from the north you should look for spots where black swamp water pours into the lowered river. This water carries minnows, crawfish, and other food through cuts and channels along the shores, and fish gather to feed at each inlet. Fish with fly, plug or bait; if you can find where black swamp water really pours in, the fishing will really be something."

As you can well imagine, I'm looking forward to the day when finally I'll have the chance to fish with Tom Nixon.

Dry Flies

Once in a while you'll see bass feeding on a hatch of insects and you can have exciting sport if you go at them with dry flies. Generally speaking, details such as pattern, size, and drag which enter into trout fishing cause rising bass relatively little concern. Toss them a floating artificial and they'll go for it, regardless of size or pattern. (Still generally speaking!) Anyway, you needn't worry about drag—dry flies usually work best on bass if you twitch them so that they skate or skitter along on the surface in hitches.

Don't conclude that you must wait for one of those infrequent rises to take bass on a dry fly, though. Some evening at dusk, tie on a bushy, high-riding dry fly in about No.-8 size, grease your line, and work the shorelines. Lay your fly on the water carefully, but forget all the other rules which apply to trout fishing with dry flies. Let the fly rest for a moment, then give it a couple of smart twitches. Wait for a strike, then if it fails to come, make your floater skate across the water for a few feet. Make it tremble with the barest perceptible motions, skim the surface in spurts, and, in general, display the unpredictable behavior of a live insect. Don't forget to give it long rests between bursts of activity, for though action may attract the bass, they frequently hold their fire until your fly becomes a sitting duck.

BASS BUGGING

Here's where you meet a fighting fish at his fighting best. Tease him with a floating bug and he'll smash the surface in a strike which will make your heart skip a few beats. Sting his jaw with the light lure's single barb and he'll bust out all over with indignation. Hear his gills rattle in that first mad leap and feel your light rod throb under his powerful surges. That's bass fishing!

Just how bass "bugs" came to be so named is far from clear, for they certainly don't resemble insects. Some imitate frogs and mice, as a matter of fact, yet all are referred to as bugs. Actually, they need not resemble anything, just as long as they float and kick up a commotion when twitched along the surface. Effective bugs include creations with bodies made of cork, balsa, plastic, and deer hair. They vary, each from the other in shape and color, but all float high on the water, all stir up a fuss when retrieved, and all take bass.

Most bass bugs have bulky bodies which offer considerable air resistance when cast. These lures—bugs made from cork or balsa—create maximum surface disturbance, attract plenty of bass as a result, but it requires a heavy, powerful rod to cast them any distance. This has led to the impression that bass bugging calls for wrist-breaking labor with a rod too stiff and heavy to handle with ease and comfort. Fortunately this is only half the story, for you'll need a heavy rod only if you stick to the wood-bodied bugs.

Deer-hair Bass Bugs

You can do your bass bugging with a four-ounce dry-fly rod by merely switching to the hair-bodied bugs. You may not get quite the sputter and burble you can wring from the dish-faced cork and balsa lures, but you can cast them a whale of a lot farther (with less effort, too) and that makes up for any shortcomings they may have. Bass find them attractive; they'll take fish alongside the bulkier bugs any day; and when you lay them out beyond range of the others, they take more.

Pattern is of minor importance in the deer-hair bugs, as it is in the other types; and most lure companies offer satisfactory models. The various hair mice and frogs all work well, as do bugs trimmed to other shapes. One of the most stream-lined and easiest to cast is the Deacon, tied on a limited scale by Roy Yates of Toledo, Ohio. The Deacon has a bullet-shaped head of closely clipped deer hair, trailing "wings" of coarse, white bucktail, and a long, forked tail consisting of two flaring yellow hackle feathers. On a four-ounce rod you can cast it almost as easily and far as a dry fly. This matter of distance deserves stressing as one of the most important tricks of bass bugging.

Long Casts

Most bass buggers make the mistake of fishing too short a line. Your bass bugs work best along shore and you can't expect to get within 20 or 30 feet of a fish lying in shallow water without putting him on his guard. Resist the temptation to do your bass bugging the easy way; instead of closing in on likely spots, work them from 50 feet out, or at least from as far out as you can reach. You'll take twice as many bass as you will with easy 30-foot casts. Makes for more work but fills the stringer.

Leaders

The heavy, hard-to-cast bass bugs encourage the use of short, coarse leaders, for they "fall off" and refuse to turn over at the end of the cast when you use a long, fine strand. With the deer-hair bugs, however, you can use leaders from six to nine feet long which taper to points as fine as IX. You'll get more strikes with such leaders in the shallow water where you'll do your bugging, and this tallies as another point in favor of the easier-to-cast hair bugs. Don't worry about handling bass on a leader tapered to IX. It only tests about three and one-half pounds, true, but grab hold of the end and let somebody "play" you with the rod. You'll be amazed at the strain you can exert with perfect safety to both leader and rod.

Fishing the Bugs

Bugging prospects start to pick up as afternoon shadows creep over the water, and they become increasingly better as dusk, the witching hour, approaches. On second thought, this had better be qualified as a generality, just as all "rules" of fishing have no hard and fast limits or precepts. Bass take bugs whenever you can find them close to shore. Generally, that's toward the end of the day, but you'll have fast and furious bass bugging at high noon if you fish often enough.

In any event, grease your line before you start, for a sinking line pulls your bug under, kills its action, and places a severe strain on your rod at the pickup. If you have both silk and nylon fly lines, choose the nylon for bass bugging, for it floats much better and longer. Dress it with a prepared floatant, rub the grease into the pores of the finish with your fingers, then remove any excess dressing with a cloth. Repeat as required.

While on the subject of lines, you may find it worth the money to invest in a forward-taper or torpedo-head for your bass bugging. By having the line weight forward, you get greater distance, and this comes as a welcome help when casting the heavier bugs. With the deer-hair numbers you can make out satisfactorily with an ordinary double taper, though it helps considerably to snip off about half of the fine end-length. The points of most double tapers are far too long for any type of fly fishing and are a particular nuisance when casting bugs.

Now, let's get at the fishing. First of all, pick a shore protected from the wind, for your bug will get in its most telling licks on a glassy surface where its slightest movement creates visible waves. If the shore is shaded, so much the better.

Creep along shore and hunt for the pockets and clues to underwater cover. See that stub lying on the bank? It extends into the water and, for all you know, branches out to form just the retreat bass love. Drop your bug near the spot where it enters the water. From way out here? What else?—you can't afford to go closer and run the risk of alarming any and all bass present.

You can't be too deliberate in your bug fishing. Wait patiently after each cast and you may get a strike before you move the bug an inch. More often, though, your wait sets the stage for a roaring attack with the first movement. Make the first twitch a good hard one to simulate a sudden dash for freedom. A bass watching the bug will hope for just such a sudden spurt to test his reflexes. Wait again if the first twitch doesn't result in a strike; maybe you've tangled with a fish who requires prolonged teasing. On the other hand, perhaps no bass was close enough to detect the bug when it dropped, but your sudden yank has called one in from a distance. At any rate, continue to rest and twitch the bug alternately through all the likely water before picking it up. You'll be rewarded by many a strike during the last few feet of the retrieve.

Casting's Fun, Too

Every cast challenges your accuracy and skill with the fly rod and this makes bass bugging a doubly interesting game. Not that this would follow if you cast only for the sake of casting, but the more often you succeed in dropping your bug in the hard-to-hit spots, the more bass you take. What's more, you get twice the thrill from raising a bass in a spot reached only by skillful casting than from a strike which occurs in open water.

You'll find that bass are generally reluctant to move far from their chosen spots to take a bug. Frequently it's a case of dropping your lure on their noses or getting nothing for your pains. Bass like to lie far back in the shadow of a tree's drooping branches, for example, but they all too seldom dash out to hit a bug worked along the edge of the trailing foliage. Sometimes you can whip your bug beneath the low-hanging branches with a side-arm cast, and more often than not you get a rousing strike whenever you penetrate the shadowy depths. Again, the branches hang so close to the water that to cast beyond them seems an impossibility. Don't give up, though, without trying this little trick:

Make a side-arm cast but don't attempt to shoot the bug through the narrow space between branches and water. Instead, aim for a point directly under the outermost limbs, keep your cast low and put plenty of drive into it. With luck, the bug will hit where you aimed, but, instead of stopping, will bounce or ricochet far back under the leafy cover. If a big bass comes up and slams into your bug you can feel the old ego start to take on new life.

Time and again you get chances to work the stunt of dangling the bug from a twig, although the opportunities come more through accident than by design. If you cast as

Casting a bass bug: the ricochet

close to good bass cover as you should, you'll be forever looping your line or leader over a branch or reed. Instead of snatching the bug back for a new cast, draw in line gently until the bug hangs in mid-air. Twitch it slightly to make it dance and you'll get one of the biggest thrills of bass bugging when a bass leaps straight up to snatch the dangling lure.

Don't overlook any opportunity to give bass the impression that the bug has either jumped or fallen from shore to the water. Lay it directly on rocks, logs, or grassy banks, then draw it into the water after a short wait. Bass watch the shorelines for any and all creatures foolish enough to leave the safety of land or unfortunate enough to tumble in. Try the same trick around pad beds; drop

Casting a bass bug: shooting for projecting branch

Casting a bass bug: pulling off a lily pad

the bug on a pad, twitch it just enough to set up tremors, then make it dive into the water.

As you can see, bugs are to the fly rod what plugs—especially the floaters—are to the bait-casting rod. Though more fishermen use the shorter rod, bass buggers make up for their lack of numbers by their enthusiasm for the fly-rod method. Individual preferences for plugging and bugging have led to spirited discussions as to which method produces the most bass, and especially which accounts for the bigger fish. Safe to say, this matter will never be settled to anybody's satisfaction.

Plug vs. Bug Contest

I know of two fishermen who once staged a contest, and as a site for the match they chose a small bass pond where both had fished frequently and knew the water intimately. Starting at 2:00 P.M. they fished for alternate 15-minute intervals until dark, the bait caster using whatever plugs he chose and the fly-rod wielder tossing bugs.

While wind and sun were on the water the plug enthusiast pulled away to an early lead with the help of deep-running lures, but as the sun sank the tide began to turn. Though the bait caster switched to surface lures and took fish, he couldn't hold to the pace set by the bugs as the match went into its final rounds. Here's how the contest wound up:

	Small bass (under 2 pounds)	Large bass (over 2 pounds)	Total
Plugs	5	4	9
Bugs	13	4	17

Looks like bugs catch more small bass than big ones, doesn't it? Wait a minute, though. Notice that at least, on this occasion, they held their own with the plugs when it came to hooking large fish. You can't prove anything by an afternoon's fishing, of course, but bass bugging and pulg casting generally seem to work out along these lines. You catch more small bass on the bugs, to be sure, but they take just about as many big fellows as the plugs.

You can release almost every bug-caught bass without harming him in the slightest, so the smaller bass you take on bugs make for livelier fishing and no damage done. In addition, you'll hook your share of heavy fish, no matter what any plug caster may tell you to the contrary.

SPINNING

Bass must have a pretty tough time of it. They must learn to steer clear of plugs, ignore those tantalizing bass bugs, and inspect each morsel of food for hidden hooks before eating it. As though all this wasn't enough, they have the whole gamut of spinning lures to contend with. It's hard to see how they can take a moment's comfort.

Spoons and Spinners

You'll find that the small metal spinning lures work as well on bass as they do on trout and probably more than one fisherman has made this discovery while spinning for trout in water which held bass. I know of one such stream where fat rainbows and scrappy river smallmouths live side by side. Though most who go there fish for trout, they take fully as many bass whenever they use the spinning rod.

Take your spinning outfit to the bass lakes and you have the answer for those plug-shy bass who merely laugh at large lures. Work from far off, use your favorite trout spoons, and you'll generally catch the bass off guard. Where trout seem to prefer the wobblers to lures with revolving blades, bass appear to like both equally well, and you may find that lures which have given poor results on trout will show up as exceptional bass killers. Along the same line, lures which are a bit too big for average-size trout will take bass of all sizes.

You can't beat spinning, either, when it comes to taking bass from deep water on artificials. Flick out your spoon or spinner in a long cast, let it sink, then keep it just off the bottom with a slow retrieve. The metal lures allow you to make exceptionally long casts, and thus enable you to cover large areas. They sink quickly and their density keeps them close to the bottom while retrieved slowly. Finally, they have bass appeal—an unbeatable combination.

Sometimes you can hurry things up in deep-water fishing by dressing up your offering with a nightcrawler. Use a lure which features a single spinner blade and has a fairly long body. Hang your crawler on the hooks so it trails behind, and berely move the spinner along to bottom. Give an occasional yank to make the blade flash, but depend on the nightcrawler's taste appeal for strikes rather than upon action. You'll get bass with this combination, and it also takes walleyes and big perch.

Bass Bugs

Bass bugging with the spinning outfit? Looks impossible at first glance, but you can do it.

Take one of those big, balsa-bodied bugs which make such a fuss on the water, drill a hole in the wood, and stuff it with two or three buckshot. Tamp plastic wood around the shot to keep them from rattling, seal the hole, and apply a coat of waterproof varnish when the plastic wood has dried.

With the shot-weighted bug you can make reasonably long casts, yet the lure remains sufficiently buoyant to float fairly high on the water. Give it the same teasing action that you would any bass bug.

Pork Chunks

We have already paid tribute to this old-timer among bass lures. If it has a fault, it lies in its rather light weight which can make casting difficult with the average bait-casting outfit. With the spinning rod you can lay a chunk out with no trouble at all, so turn to this old reliable when you want a surface spinning lure which really produces.

Full-size Bass Lures?

You can cast heavy plugs on your spinning rod—cast them a mile, as a matter of fact—but you'd better let spinning take over only where bait casting leaves off. It takes a good, solid jolt to set those big hooks in the jaw of a bass, and you need the stiffness of a bait-casting road and a line stronger than the monofilament to do the job properly. Besides, the big plugs and lures put an unhealthy strain on the spinning rod which is bound to take its toll if you use them long enough.

Use the spinning rod with light lures and let the bait-casting rod perform the heavy duties.

Skittering for Bass

Everybody knows how pickerel go for a skittered fish belly, but not nearly as many realize that skittering takes, bass, too, especially largemouths. Skittering has been done for years with cane poles and fly rods but the spinning rod makes a better skittering tool than either.

You can slice a skittering bait from the belly of a perch. Start at the vent and cut out the section which includes the ventral fins. This gives you a spoon-shaped strip with the reddish fins adding a dash of color. Shove the barb of a 2/0 hook through the strip between the two fins and cast along the edges of pad beds, over weeds, and into all other shallow-water retreats likely to hold bass. Let the strip sink a bit after the cast, then bring it back with a series of jerks. Slack off immediately when you get a strike, for the fish probably has the strip only partly in his mouth. Give him time to gulp it in before you set the hook.

If pickerel or pike share quarters with the bass, you'll take these fellows too, of course. Even though you hold out for bass, save at least one of the pickerel as a source of belly strips superior to the perch baits. Cut a four-inch strip from the white belly, taper it to a point, and shave the flesh from the tapered end until you have a tail consisting of little more than skin. The waving tail, plus the greater flexibility of the entire strip, gives you more action than the perch belly and this brings more strikes.

NIGHT FISHING

The toughest part of fishing for bass at night is getting started. Probably every bass fisherman knows that bass feed throughout the night, but hardly one in 50 actually carries through with a plan to fish after dark. It simply doesn't seem like a sensible thing to do. It isn't. But it's fun.

You'll Take Bass

Darkness puts bass on the prowl. They leave their daytime retreats, cruise the shorelines for food, and are inclined to snap up anything that moves. Though they apparently see surprisingly well on even the blackest night, they tend to be less critical, so you can use shorter, heavier leaders and make shorter casts than during hours of daylight.

Surface lures shape up as your best bet for afterdark fishing. Twitch a floating plug or bass bug along the surface and you'll bring nearby bass racing to investigate the cause of the disturbance. More often than not, they'll pile into it with little hesitation. The fact that they're on the hunt and need little teasing swings the odds in your favor when you fish at night.

You'll probably have less trouble if you stick to the fly rod. Bass bugs don't hang as readily in the brush as do plugs with their multiple hooks. With the fly rod you'll also avoid backlashes, the curse of nighttime bait casting.

Whether plugging or bugging, stick close to shore, move slowly, and cover the water methodically. You can expect to find bass anywhere in shallow water, so don't concentrate on the spots where you find fish during the daytime. They spread all over the place at night and you'll take fish where you wouldn't think of fishing during the day. Sandy beaches where swimmers cavort daily will yield bass at night, even though the bottom offers absolutely nothing by way of cover.

Step up the action of your surface lures at night. Fish them with the same twitching retrieve, but don't wait as long between twitches. You'll attract more bass that way, and once they see or hear your lure, they need but little provocation to strike.

In spite of the temptation to choose a night when a full moon aids visibility, pick a darker night for the best bass fishing. The blacker it is, the better the bass seem to like it. Let your eyes become adjusted and you can see after a fashion in what at first appears to be pitch darkness.

6. Lake Trout and Salmon

LAKE TROUT SEEM TO THINK THAT THEY CAN LIVE only in water which is around 45 degrees Fahrenheit, and nobody can talk them out of this ridiculous idea. For all they know they might like a temperature of 60 degrees better, once they got used to it.

This finicky trait costs us a lot of good fishing, for lakers offer sport on light tackle only when they lie in shallow water. For a few short weeks in early spring and late fall they find the surface temperature to their liking and they then hang near the top. That's the time to hit them for the most fun.

Fly Fishing

You don't normally think in terms of fly fishing on days when ice forms in the guides and your hands turn blue, but you may have to put up with rugged weather if you want to take lake trout on flies. As soon as the lakes clear of ice, lakers come close to shore, hungry and ready to snap up anything which resembles a smelt or minnow. They won't stay there long, so you'd better brave the cold if you want some exciting streamer and bucktail fishing, with fish averaging maybe four pounds and running to ten or better.

Use the rod and line which you ordinarily do for streamer fishing, but splice a generous amount of backing to the fly line, just in case. Your leader doesn't have to be tapered, and a length of nine feet is plenty. Going finer than four-pound test won't get you any more fish, and may lose some for you.

All streamer and bucktail patterns will take lakers, but you'll do well to stick with such proven numbers as the Gray Ghost, Black Ghost, Supervisor, and Dark Edson Tiger. Flies with two hooks in tandem are the surest hookers. No.-4 is a popular size for lakers.

Pick a rocky shoreline and let your fly sink into the deeper pockets, pinching on a split shot or two to help sink it if necessary. Remember that you're trying to imitate a smelt or minnow and that your fly will do that best if it runs well under the surface. Retrieve at moderate speed, working your rod to give the fly a darting, smeltlike action. Keep moving to cover as much water as possible. Lakers are hungry in the spring and don't require much teasing, so you'll only waste time by casting away in one spot.

On calm evenings you can sometimes spot lakers rolling at the surface, and cast directly to rising fish, but generally you have to go at it "blind." This makes slow work of it and you almost always can turn up more lakers if you troll your flies or, better yet, combine trolling and casting. We'll have more to say about fly trolling when we get to landlocked salmon; just remember that it is just as effective on lakers as it is on landlocks.

Bait Casting and Spinning

If bait casting or spinning's your game, you can get in your licks with spoons and wobblers while the lakers are near the top. Maybe you'll find that they have it over flies, for you can sink the metal lures deeper than you can the streamers and pick up fish when they're just a little too far down for fly fishing.

Good spoons for lakers are those of medium size which you can handle on either a bait casting rod or a fairly stiff spinning rod. Almost any metal wobbler will take lake trout, but if you have any doubts you can always snap on a Dardevle and know that you have picked a time-tested lure.

The way you fish counts for more than your choice of lure, just as it does in all kinds of fishing. Probably the worst mistake you can make is to get in the rut of retrieving in the same old way, cast after cast. Vary the action; run your lure close to the bottom by letting it sink after each cast, then reeling slowly. If this doesn't work, try reeling faster. This makes your lure angle toward the top, so pause every ten feet to let it flutter back down and regain depth. Try as many combinations of reeling and rod twitching as you can think of. Experiment until you get results, then feed them more of the same.

Deep Trolling

Trolling for lake trout after they have returned to deep water is looked on by many as the dullest occupation known to man, yet others find it fascinating. Probably those who like it are the ones who have taken the trouble to learn the business. It can be discouraging at the start and it's not at all surprising that so many lack the patience to see it through.

Since lakers stubbornly refuse to live in water much warmer than 45 degrees, and prefer it closer to 40, you're faced with the job of locating water this cool, even on the hottest summer days. If the surface temperature has gone no higher than 60 degrees you can generally hit your layer of trout water by going down 40 feet or so. That's not so bad, but when the surface warms to 70 or 80 degrees, as it does in many lakes by midsummer, you may have to go as deep as 80 or 100 feet, and sometimes even deeper!

With a "maximum-minimum" thermometer you can locate the water that holds the lakers, but that's only part of the job. It's one thing to know that the trout are 80 feet down, and another to get your lure down to them and hold it there while you troll.

A braided fiber line—silk, nylon, etc.—is not satisfactory for deep trolling. You must hang on an appalling amount of lead to hold the lure down where you want it, and, even then, the line develops such a belly that it makes the hooking of striking fish extremely uncertain. Metal lines, on the other hand, sink of their own accord and pass through the water with but slight friction resulting. They develop very little belly, and the hooks sink home when a fish strikes, due to the straight pull against the rod.

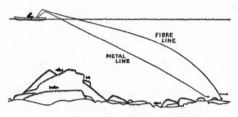

Action of fiber and metal lines in deep trolling

The depth at which you troll should determine the type of metal line you select. To fish moderately deep you can use a braided or twisted metal line and enjoy the greater ease with which these two types handle, for they do not tend to kink, coil, and spring as does a line of solid wire. Due to their lesser density, however, they do not sink as readily as a solid strand, and the latter makes a more suitable line when you must go down a hundred feet or more to take fish. You must use care in letting out, spooling, and handling these lines in general, for a "bird's nest" of this fine wire cuts deeply into a man's soul, then proceeds to rub salt in the wound. Sensible caution will spare you this pain, however, and the resulting advantages are cheaply bought for the relatively slight risk you run of a tangle.

Lines of Monel metal have by now won the nod of favor from the majority of deep-water fishermen, and Monel is especially preferred in the solid wire class. Monel wire is extremely strong for its diameter, and, by using a line that tests around 15 pounds, it is possible (and practical) to use an ordinary bait casting outfit to troll at great depths with those lures that do not place undue strain on the rod. Lines of greater strength—25- to 35-pound test—are also surprisingly fine and you need no greatly oversized reels to hold all you need for the deepest trolling—200 yards or so. Monel does not kink with disastrous results (as does copper) nor does it rust or otherwise deteriorate with use.

To those who object to deep trolling on the grounds that it requires tackle so heavy that it robs the game of sport, the fine-gauge Monel lines now available offer a possible solution. A fly reel will hold several hundred yards of the five-pound test, and this hair-fine line will take a streamer or bucktail down to the deepest levels without straining a four- or five-ounce fly rod in the least. Thus it is possible to take lakers from the depths on the lightest of tackle, although working a heavy fish to the surface from over 100 feet down may prove to be a long, drawn-out process.

A solid wire line has one characteristic which you should keep in mind when a fish is first hooked: it will not stretch. While this feature makes for sure hooking, it also gives a fish a good opportunity to tear free during that first wild flurry if you handle him with a heavy hand. Don't snub him short during those first few moments, especially if your rod is on the stiff and heavy side.

The closer to the bottom you troll your lure, the better, for that's where the lakers generally lie. Here's one way to do it:

Snap on a wobbler that rides with the single, fixed hook upward, such as the Pfleuger Record Spoon. Fish the spoon as is, or hang a thin fluttering tail of pork rind on to the hook. Slow down to trolling speed—just fast enough to "work" the spoon—and start paying out line (not too fast with that single-strand wire!). Eventually you'll feel the spoon bump bottom, for this will kill the throbbing action momentarily. As soon as the spoon touches, slip a glove on your right hand and grasp the line, laying the rod beside you or propping it between your knees. Reach straight behind you, then sweep your arm forward along the gunwale through an arc of nearly 180°, repeating the motion with a steady rhythm. The forward sweep picks the lure from close to bottom and makes it dart upward, then, when you bring your arm back, it slows and flutters downward. If you feel it brush bottom every few times, you're working it just right. The resulting action is of the sort likely to provoke strikes, and by sounding the depth constantly, you hold your lure at its most effective level.

You can work this stunt where the lake floor is relatively clean, but you soon come to grief if you attempt it over ledges or in other spots where your spoon will hang up. Neither can you bump lures with treble hooks along the bottom without snagging constantly or picking up debris from the bottom. Here's a way to keep your lure in the clear and feel out the bottom at the same time.

To the end of your wire line attach a barrel swivel and fit this in turn to a fairly large split ring. Take about 3 feet of bait casting line, tie a 6-ounce bell sinker to one end, a swivel to the other, and work this swivel into the split ring. Next you need a 10-foot length of 20-pound test nylon. Rig your lure to one end and swivel the other to the split ring.

Now you have a three-way rig—the nylon angles away from the metal line at the split ring, letting your lure run close to the bottom but never quite touching it. With this type of rig you maintain contact with the bottom through the lead sinker, but without fear of the lure snagging or fouling. To fish light lures, or those with a pronounced tendency to plane, as close to the bottom as possible you may need to shorten the sinker line and add length to your

Method of fishing for landlocked salmon

nylon leader. Heavy lures may require just the opposite to keep them from hanging up. Trial and error will soon point the way.

Practically all wobblers and spoons make good trolling lures, and a jointed plug will take its share of lakers. Floating plugs (divers, not surface plugs, of course) almost never snag bottom when properly adjusted behind a sinker, for they dip down only when under way, and rise when you slacken speed or stop for any reason.

A combination of bait and hardware is the favorite of many lake fishermen—a sewn minnow, a smelt, or a gob of crawlers behind a single spinner or the tandem blades of the Dave Davis rig. No matter what you hang on your line, however, get it down deep and keep it there, for that's 90 percent of the secret of taking lakers after they have left the surface.

LANDLOCKED SALMON

So many have sung the praises of landlocked salmon that it's a wonder that the lot of them haven't developed swelled heads. Beautiful to look at, and swift, slashing fighters, land-locks deserve everything good that's been said about them, but they're not quite so aristocratic as they're often made out. My first chance at landlocked salmon came when I was too young to hold them in any reverence. Fishing from shore with a battered telescope rod, I took them on nightcrawlers almost as easily as you'd catch perch. Since then, of course, I have learned better than to use such crude methods on so noble a fish. Besides, I rather doubt that worms would work as well now as they did years ago.

Fly Fishing

Landlocked salmon, like lake trout, come close to the surface only when the water is cold. Early in the spring, and again in the fall, they come into the shallows along the shorelines where they afford some of the most exciting light-tackle fishing you can get in fresh water. Far and away the most popular way to take them at that time is by fly-rod trolling.

The rig: A fly rod—better make it a stick of at least four ounces—a silk line that sinks readily, an eight- or nine-foot level leader of four- or six-pound test, a streamer for a tail fly, and another as a dropper about four feet up the leader.

Here's a suggestion on choosing your patterns: Popular theory has it that your flies should imitate smelt, but don't take this too literally. True enough, smeltlike flies like the Green Ghost and Nine-Three are salmon killers, but many times

Three-way rig for deep trolling

such patterns as the Dark Edson Tiger or Mickey Finn will bring you more strikes, although neither looks anything like a smelt. It's wise to offer salmon a choice; tie on a smeltlike pattern for a tail fly and a contrasting number as a dropper.

Another tip: Try trolling a red and white wobbler in the tiny fly-rod size. Very deadly! Do salmon take *this* for a smelt? If they do they should have their eyes examined!

A bang-up job of salmon trolling really calls for a two- man crew. Work it something like this:

Troll a long line and a short one. Strip 50 to 90 feet from one reel and 20 to 30 from the other. If a salmon resists the urge to nail the first flies, the next pair may win him over a few seconds later.

When you have both lines out, one of the crew should rig up a third rod and cast toward shore. Maybe he'll pick up a fish, maybe not; his big job is to keep shooting his fly close to shore to toll fish out of the pockets so they'll see your trolled flies and smack them. If he lifts his fly before it has swung directly astern and into the path of the oncoming streamers, he deserves a chewing out—see that he gets it!

The harder the wind blows, the more salmon fodder the waves pound up along shore, and the hotter the fishing. Salmon move right into the surf to feed, especially where large rocks or boulders give them partial protection from the tossing water. Give such shorelines your attention and pay particular heed to any point which sends out a reef or bar which the waves break over. Shame on you if you give a hot spot like that only one try. Bring your boat around—the pounding will help settle your breakfast—and drag through that rich pay dirt again, then swing back through at least once more before you move on.

Very important: Troll fast for landlocked salmon! They're swift, powerful swimmers and wide-ranging cruisers who like an excuse to show their speed. To excite them, your flies must move!

More good business: Twiggle! Saw the line back and forth through the guides to make the flies dart ahead and fall back. A big help any time, but look on twiggling as a must when working a likely spot for all there is in it.

You pray for a good, heavy chop, so what do you get? A flat calm, of course, not so good for salmon fishing, but here are a few things to try when the water is glassy smooth:

Troll a very long line, going well into your backing before you stop stripping. If this doesn't pay off, shorten up until your flies hang in the wash of the motor! Won't the motor scare them? No! The propeller acts as an attractor, and that's the point of the trick.

If your partner hooks a fish, grab the extra rod and start casting. Nothing excites a salmon more than to see one of his mates dashing madly about with a fly stuck in his jaw. If the hooked fish has attracted another, he's likely to snap up your fly out of envy the moment he sees it. You risk a tangle, of course, but who wouldn't for a twin killing?

Spinners and Spoons

You can take landlocked salmon by casting spoons and wobblers as you do for lake trout. Lures of bait-casting weight will turn the trick, or you can spin-fish with the smaller lures and get good results. Tie on the same lures for trolling or run a minnow or smelt ahead of one of the standard spinner rigs.

But before you turn to hardware, give the fly rod and streamers a thorough try. Even though the metal lures may have a slight edge over flies—many will hotly deny that they do!—they call for stiff rods which cheat you of thrills once you have your salmon hooked. Sample this incomparable fighter and leaper on four or five ounces of fly rod, then see if you would have it any other way!

Deep Trolling

Hot weather drives the salmon into deep water where you can reach them only by resorting to the methods recommended for lake trout. They come mighty hard, once they leave the surface, and to take them requires the same patience and study that makes lake-trout trolling too much of a chore for many. All the lake-trout lures will do for salmon but probably the most popular lure is the Dave Davis spinner rig followed by a sewn minnow or smelt.

ATLANTIC SALMON

When the dreamed-of day comes and you shoot the works on your first trip to a salmon river, you'll have very little know-how that carries over to salmon fishing. Aside from the purely mechanical skills, it's actually best to forget all you've learned about fishing.

Forget About Trout!

If you don't, you'll size up the water in terms of trout from force of habit . . . and invariably come to the wrong conclusions!

You won't find salmon where you'd expect to find trout for two good reasons: Salmon in fresh water show little interest in food, and they seek no cover. Spots which attract trout on both counts hold no appeal for salmon. Unless you remember that, you may spend a good share of your time casting to all the wrong places.

And Rely on Your Guide!

He's the fellow who can keep you from pounding away where you'll do yourself no good. He knows his river—the pools which hold fish, and the precise spots in those pools where the fish lie. Added to this, he can see a salmon that you can't make out to save your life. Put your fly where he tells you to!

Fly Fishing, Period!

You have no choice but to fly-fish for Atlantic salmon, for no other method is legal in North American rivers. This makes a tough proposition tougher, for you're restricted to bits of feathers and fur in teasing strikes from fish who have sworn off eating! Most would applaud this restriction, however, even if it were not needed as a sound conservation measure. Held to a fly rod, you're bound to get your money's worth when you hook a salmon. And then some!

Wet-fly Fishing

Salmon fishing has inspired fly tyers to their greatest efforts, resulting in such exquisitely beautiful patterns as the Jock Scott, Durham Ranger, and Silver Doctor. Though these, and equally colorful favorites, have won well-deserved reputations, one can't but wonder if their elaborate construction is an actual requirement.

Many fishermen have toyed with this idea, and some have had the courage to break with tradition and use simple patterns. Results seem to prove that ordinary bucktails, streamers, and wet flies will take as many salmon as the fancy creations. This doesn't knock the gaudy "standards" out of the running, but it shows that you'll do all right with a well-stocked book of trout flies.

As it does in most fly fishing, size of hooks seems to play a more important role than pattern. Flies tied on Nos. 4, 6, and 8 come in for the most use, but you should have some larger ones with you for possible high-water fishing. When rivers are low you need to swing to the opposite end of the scale, but there's a limit to how small you can go on hook size without killing your chances of landing such powerful fish. You can get around this obstacle by using low-water salmon flies—flies with bodies small enough to win over critical fish, but tied on hooks large enough to hold.

Why salmon rise to a fly at all is a mystery, for they leave their appetites behind them in salt water. They certainly must rise for a reason, though, so let's assume that the sight of your fly fans to life some lingering spark of the feeding instinct. This still leaves you the job of begging strikes from fish that aren't hungry, but we'll do our best to give you a little leverage with the following tips.

Hottest fishing comes with the rising water that follows a heavy rain. Fresh fish come into the river and those already there show more interest in flies. You can't order the rain, but you can be up bright and early the morning after any comes.

Keep your eyes peeled for rolling fish—not leapers, for leaping fish are poor bets, but "porpoising" salmon who break the surface with their backs. These are your hottest prospects, so work on any you see.

Locating a salmon, and then pegging away at him, is ever so much better than fishing blind. Blind casting will win you grilse—small salmon who come into the river after but a single year in the sea—but your best chance of hooking a mature salmon of ten pounds or better comes with finding your fish first, then going to work on him. Cast to him repeatedly; he may finally get the urge to rise, or he may take a crack at your fly out of sheer annoyance. If he shifts his position when your fly comes over him, you've got him interested and you should get set for a rise.

If he rises and misses—or you miss him!—get your fly back to him quickly to give him a second chance. If he refuses, change to a different pattern, one size smaller, and try him with that. Make sure that you have him relocated after a rise, for he may drop downstream when he settles back.

Before you give up on a fish, try this: Get directly upstream from him if you can, then let your fly hang in the current in front of him. Draw it ahead, let it fall back, make it shimmy; he may tear into it when you have his nerves worn thin.

Under ordinary circumstances, cast cross-stream and bring your fly back slowly and smoothly, holding it close to the top. Here again, you'll do well to forget about trout fishing, for a fly which swims evenly seems to bring more strikes than one fished with a darting "trout" action.

If you have no luck with the swimming retrieve, try drifting your fly. Cast cross-stream as before, but then keep your line as slack as possible by constant mending. This lets your fly drift sideways under no tension and sometimes brings up a salmon when a moving fly fails.

Remember the "riffling fly" trick mentioned in Chapter 2? It takes trout, but its chief claim to fame is as a salmon persuader. Tie fly to leader with the usual Turle knot, then half-hitch the leader just back of the head of the fly so it comes away from the under side of the shank at an angle. Riffle the fly by planing it smoothly along the surface on a short, taut line. If you can see a wake behind it, you're cutting the right caper. Paste a big, bright star opposite this stunt; it's a real fish-taker and you don't want to risk forgetting it.

Sometimes you wind up farther ahead if you "rest" a pool during the afternoon, then work it over during the last hour of fishing. Late afternoon is one of the best times to raise salmon, and they're all the more likely to strike if they haven't seen a fly for several hours.

Above all, heed the advice of your guide. Each salmon river has secrets and quirks known only to him and others like him who study the stream year after year. He'll put all his know-how to work for you, for he has a reputation to maintain and is as eager to see you fast to a salmon as you are to hook one. Treat what he says as the law!

Dry-fly Fishing

Although wet-fly fishing is the most popular method, dry flies have an important place in salmon fishing. They are especially effective when the water is low and warm and the fish have been in the river for some time. Make sure you have a supply with you on any salmon-fishing trip, but particularly if you go late in the season.

The most popular patterns run to such bushy high-floaters as the bivisibles and hair-winged Wulffs, but some fishermen stick with their favorite trout patterns and take salmon on Quill Gordons, Cahills, and the like. The most effective size depends on water conditions and the whims of the fish. Salmon fresh from the sea may rise to a large dry fly—a No. 6, for example—while later on they may hold out for something tiny. Here again, you should trim larger flies, or use the low-water type, to avoid using hooks too small to hold your fish.

You can't comb the water with a dry fly as you can with a wet, so it's even more important to zero in on a particular fish when dry-fly fishing. Cast well above him to give him a good, long look at your fly before it reaches him. With plenty of time to make up his mind he may rise and take it, whereas he'll probably refuse it if you drop it on his nose and force him to a hurried decision.

If your best dragless floats come to naught, try twitching the fly along the surface. If you can get above your fish, float your fly down to him, skitter it back upstream a few feet, then let it drift down again. A little action may be all that's needed to draw a strike.

Hooking

Your trout-fishing habits will do you dirt at this critical point, too, if you don't watch yourself. Due to his bulk, a salmon makes a hair-raising boil as he comes for your fly. If you follow your natural inclination, you'll strike too soon and yank the fly away from him. Give him time to clamp the fly in his jaws, then set the hook as he takes it down. Compared to trout, salmon are slow in ejecting a fly, so you run little risk of striking too late. It takes a high order of self-control to hold fast while a great shape rolls up behind your fly, takes it in his mouth, and sinks back with it . . . but that's the way to hook salmon.

Playing

You can't possibly lick a salmon with anything as puny as a fly rod. The spring of the bamboo will wear down lesser fish, but to a fear-crazed salmon it is as nothing. All you can do is hang on while he licks himself!

You have your job cut out for you to stick with him while he burns up his tremendous energy in long runs and wild leaps. He'll show you such power as you'll see in no other fish in fresh water, and you have but to give him leverage for a fleeting instant to have him break free. Give him his head and let him rip; the longer and faster his runs, the sooner he'll tire to the point where you can at last control him with the rod and land him. Stand ready to follow him upstream or down; sometimes a quick sprint is the only way to keep him from cleaning you when he takes the bit in his teeth.

Try to remember this very important tip: Lower your rod quickly when your fish leaps or, even better, lean forward and flip as much slack at him as you can manage. If you let him jump on a tight line, he may snap the leader by a direct jerk against the reel, part it with a flirt of his powerful tail, or crash down on it with the same result. If you haul back and let him break away, don't say I didn't warn you.

You must, of course, play salmon directly from the reel. Most right-handed fly fishermen reel with their right hands, but it makes more sense to do the job with the left and leave the right hand free to handle the rod. Left-handed reeling becomes second nature with but a little practice, and you'll find it a big help in playing heavy fish on a fly rod.

Rods and Reels

The trend in salmon fishing is definitely toward lighter rods. Each year more and more salmon fishermen show up with trout rods and proceed to prove that a competent fisherman can tackle a salmon with a five-ounce, nine-foot rod and come off with a whole hide. If your fishing calls for exceptionally long casts, you may need a powerful 12-footer with double grip, but on all but the largest rivers you'll take more pleasure, and as many fish, with a shorter, lighter rod.

Unlike trout reels, which serve as little more than line-holders, a salmon reel plays an important part in landing fish, much depending on its ability to run smoothly under the salmon's long, fast dashes. This calls for expert design, machining, and fitting, and rules out the possibility of salmon reels which are both satisfactory and cheap.

Pick a reel—a single action—with a narrow spool but one deep enough to hold at least 100 yards of backing under your fly line. A hundred yards—300 feet! That should give you an idea of what to expect from an Atlantic salmon!

You never know what a taste of these big fish on a fly rod will do to a fellow. I knew one trout fisherman who swore off trout fishing for life as soon as he caught his first salmon. So far, he has stuck to it—claims he can no longer get a kick out of catching a mere trout.

In contrast, there's the fishing nut I know who recently spent two thrill-packed weeks on a salmon river. As nearly as any man can, he'd had it, but it took less than a week for the old itch to creep up on him again. The following Saturday, he was out after bluegills! Said he had just as much fun with them as he ever did.

The bug never really bit that first fellow—just nipped him a little. Like the chap who held that there was no such thing as poor liquor, the true fisherman never gets his fill. He'll fish for anything that grows fins—any time, any place!

7. Pickerel, Pike, and Muskellunge

YOU CAN'T MISTAKE THE MEMBERS OF THIS TRIBE. All have the same long, racy lines, common fin arrangement, and a formidable array of sharp teeth. All the pike look so much alike, in fact, that some have difficulty telling a northern from a pickerel or a muskellunge.

Chain pickerel get their name from their body markings—a chainlike pattern of green tracings over a background of yellow. Northern pike reverse this color scheme with grayish yellow spots against a field of green. Muskellunge have the least coloration. They may show vertical stripes or bars, or they may have none at all.

For positive identification, examine cheeks and gill covers. The pickerel has a complete covering of scales over both parts, the northern has scales covering the cheeks and the upper halves of the gill covers, while the muskellunge has scales only on the top halves of each.

*Identification by means of scale patterns. From
left to right: pickerel, pike, muskellunge*

Heavyweight honors go to the muskie. These bruisers grow *big!* Muskellunge crowding 70 pounds have been taken on rod and reel, suggesting the possibility that some may attain the awesome weight of 100 pounds. Northern pike run up to 40 pounds, and 20-pounders almost always show up wherever northerns abound. Pickerel never reach comparable size. The present world's record stands at an even nine pounds, and a four-pounder is a whopper in any water.

But pickerel more than make up for their lack of size by their wide distribution and general availability. Besides, their average weight will shape up as respectable indeed, if we think in terms of bass and trout.

PICKEREL

One of the oddest pickerel-catching incidents of all time came about purely by accident. A youngster, celebrating the Fourth of July on the shore of a pond, touched a match to a firecracker and pitched it into the water. The fuse spluttered, the firecracker spun crazily, and a huge pickerel swirled up and gulped the cracker just as it exploded. Imagine the kid's surprise.

Imagine the pickerel's.

Live Bait

Forget all about worms, nymphs, crickets, grasshoppers, and such baits when you go after pickerel. They want fish, and no fooling. You'll catch an occasional pickerel on a nightcrawler or crawfish, but don't count on it. No natural bait takes as many pickerel as minnows or other small fish.

And they like fresh meat just as well when they grow up. I once rowed ashore to eat lunch and, to keep my supply of minnows lively, removed the inner section from the bait bucket and let it rest on bottom at the water's edge. Minutes later I heard an odd ponging sound. Investigating, I found a large pickerel determinedly trying to chew his way through the metal mesh of the minnow-bucket section.

This little incident leads to some interesting speculation. First, it suggests that pickerel can track down a concentration of minnows, for the minnow bucket rested on a sandy beach, many yards from weeds or other cover of any kind. From this it's easy to conclude that a minnow trap, loaded with live minnows and hung from your boat, won't hurt your chances in the least. Just try it and see!

Best Baits

Good: All small bait fish.
Better: Common shiners and golden shiners.
Best: Small yellow perch!

No question about it, if you want big pickerel. Perch won't bring you as many strikes as minnows, but they'll take more whoppers. And though you can't buy them generally, they're really not hard to come by. Fish close to shore in shallow, weedy water and you can almost always pick up a few on a No.-12 hook, baited with a dab of worm. Any under five inches are pickerel bait.

Best Size

If you happen to have a three-pound pickerel handy, open his mouth wide and look at the size of it. He could swallow himself, if he could just get into position. You might think that only huge baits would attract fish with a mouth that size, but you'll get best returns if you use minnows four to five inches long. With a ten-inch sucker, you might eventually catch a monster pickerel, but you could catch him as easily on medium-size bait, and pick up many smaller ones in the process. With the four- or five-inchers you get faster action and wind up with as many big fish.

If you suspect that your minnows are too small, try a matched pair on your hook. Try it anyway, if things slow down, for it's always a good stunt.

Still-fishing

Pickerel lurk almost everywhere you find weeds, but the deep-sunken beds make the best spots for still-fishing.

Explore the outer fringes of weed beds, and you'll find that they often extend to depths of 12 feet or more. Make these outer limits your first choice. Shallow-water pickerel cover is easy to spot and, as a result, the pad-grown bays and visible weed patches get a thorough combing. The deeper haunts come in for far less fishing and yield bigger pickerel, and more of them.

You may get a strike the moment you lower a minnow, but it's generally the smaller fish who take immediately. Large pickerel seldom dash out and grab a bait the instant they see it, so it pays to fish out each spot. You may go fishless for a half-hour, then hook a four-pounder who watched your minnow from the time you dropped it overboard.

Many fishermen fail to take as many pickerel as they should, simply because they persist in fishing their minnows above the weeds. Whenever you have no luck at this level, clamp on a heavier sinker and lower your bait into the weedy tangle. Don't jump to the conclusion that pickerel won't find your minnow, once it's "hidden" in the weeds. Remember that fish locate food with perfect ease on the darkest nights (pickerel, however, are not night feeders) and in water so roily that visibility shrinks to almost nothing. Fishing in the weeds isn't as pleasant as holding the bait just above them, but it will bring you more than one big pickerel too cagey to leave his hiding place.

Due to the pickerel's habit of looking over a minnow at great length, it's best to let the bait rest in one spot for longer periods than while bass fishing, for example. The minnow should wiggle constantly, however, so twitch the line occasionally to keep him struggling. If you have a bait which needs no prodding, strip some slack from the reel and prop the rod on the gunwale. Keep hands off, and the line may start snaking out through the guides sooner than you had hoped for.

But suppose nothing happens and you reel that you must recast, if for no other reason than to relieve the monotony. Before you haul in, try this simple stunt:

Quickly raise the minnow a couple of feet, then drop it back. No matter how long you have waited, you may draw the bait away from a pickerel on the verge of taking if you strip it in quickly. On the other hand, the threat of escape may result in a prompt strike, so run this little test before retrieving after a long, unproductive wait.

Minnows and Spinners

Pickerel probably make a deliberate inspection of a still-fished minnow because they realize that they can seize it any time they get ready. But they can make up their minds in a hurry if they have to, and you often can provoke more strikes by trolling a minnow than by still-fishing it. Merely a sewn minnow will take fish, but a combination of minnow and spinner does a much better job. Here's one of the best rigs of this type:

Use a willow-leaf blade four or five inches long which is held away from the shaft by a support of stiff wire. Tie a 4/0 hook to a 12-inch length of ten-pound test nylon and whip a No. 6–hook to the strand about three inches above. Hook a live minnow through both lips with the small hook, bind the large hook to the minnow's body with a tiny rubber band, and attach the snell behind the spinner. The trick of fishing this lure successfully lies in rowing just fast enough to keep the spinner above the weeds. If you allow the boat to glide almost to a stop between strokes, you'll travel at about the correct pace. The long, thin spinner blade turns under the slightest motion, giving off plenty of flash even though you barely move the boat.

I once knew an old-timer who fished this way exclusively. The badge of his success was the large market basket which he always carried as a creel. Most of the pickerel he caught wouldn't fit in anything smaller!

Minnow trolling rig for pickerel

Frogs

Use them for still-fishing whenever you can't get minnows. Put on enough lead to take the frog down, hook him through both lips, and fish him as you would a minnow. Use the medium-size chaps—neither the big, green fellows, nor the tiny leapers. If you can't get these, pick the very small size over the large ones.

Though frogs rate below minnows as pickerel bait in fairly deep water, they make an ideal bait for shallow-water fishing. Let them swim at the top over weed beds, near lily pads, and along the edges of rushes.

Setting the Hook

Give a pickerel plenty of time and he'll generally have the bait in his mouth where the hook will sink home. He seldom moves off with any speed once he grabs your bait, and rarely goes more than a few yards. Feed him plenty of slack and he'll go about the business of swallowing a minnow or frog without suspicion. In the process he may drop the bait to grab it in a different position, so you run the risk of a miss if you yank too soon. Let him chew for a couple of minutes, draw in any slack line gently, then hit him good and hard. A pickerel's mouth runs mainly to gristle and cartilage, so it takes a solid jerk to bury the barb.

Skittering

Modern artificial lures have gradually crowded this ancient but honorable method of pickerel fishing into the background, but you still can't beat it for fun and you can't beat it for fish. Whether you cast with a cane pole, fly rod, or spinning rod, you get the same thrill when a pickerel charges out of the weeds and overhauls your skittered bait. And you'll search hard to find a method that will take more pickerel on a day-in-day-out basis.

What makes the best skittering bait? Many old-timers would vote for a strip cut from another pickerel. They'd tell you to use a strip of the white belly on dark days, and a slab sliced from the side or back on bright days. But you can cut a bait from a pickerel and have nothing but a hunk of meat, or you can turn out a strip which flutters with the enticing action you need to get strikes. Half the secret of skittering lies in cutting the bait.

Start with a slab about four inches long, lay it flat on the blade of an oar or the boat seat, then trim it carefully to a point, tapering from a three-quarter-inch width. Now, to give the strip a pliant tail with a fishlike wiggle, shave the flesh from the tip until you have little left but skin. Round off the wide end to a blunt point and shove the barb of your hook completely through the rounded "head."

A perch belly also deserves credit as a proven skittering bait. Cut from vent to just ahead of the ventral fins and hook the bait between the fins. A dead frog of medium size probably should rate third. Hook frogs through both lips for skittering as you do for still-fishing. A strip of prepared pork rind will bring strikes, but pickerel soon drop this lure, whereas they hold and swallow the others. A good way to get around this is to rig a pair of hooks in tandem for your pork rind, and set the hook with the strike.

The technique of skittering you can deduce easily from the name. Lob your strip or frog into pockets among weeds and lily pads, then retrieve with a jerky motion at a fairly rapid speed. Slack off the moment a pickerel swirls at the bait, for he'll probably grab it by the tail end. Give him free line while he moves off with the bait, allow him a couple of minutes to get the entire strip in his mouth, then set the hook with a strong jerk.

The term "skittering" brands the technique as strictly a shallow-water method, but don't let the name mislead you. That wiggling strip of fish will take pickerel from deep water if you sink it down to them, so don't call a halt to your skittering until you have tried the sunken weed beds. Let the strip settle, then "skitter" it just above the tops of the weeds. You'll often strike days when deep "skittering" will bring far more strikes than your best efforts near shore.

Even if you find no takers, shallow or deep, remember that no real fisherman gives up without a struggle. Maybe a little more action in the bait will stir them up, so split your strip down the middle for half its length, giving it two wiggling tails instead of one. Or maybe they want color—thread some strands of bright red yarn through a white belly strip. Flash and glitter? Run a small spinner ahead of the lure—no law says you can't, and the bit of hardware may prove just what's needed.

Weedless hooks make for easier skittering; but if you lack the manufactured variety, you can make a satisfactory substitute from an ordinary hook and a small rubber band. Pull a short loop through the eye of the hook, thread the longer

Improvised weedless hook

loop through the small one, then catch it behind the barb. The taut strands help to ward off weeds but don't interfere with hooking when you get a strike.

Bait Casting

Pickerel will strike almost any casting lure you snap to your line, but some do a much better job than others. Spoons and metal wobblers generally outfish plugs and, if you were held to but a single pickerel lure, you couldn't make a better choice than the Eppinger Dardevle. In its most popular pattern of red and white, this wobbler makes a hard-to-beat choice, but you can do even better by building up a supply of these lethal spoons in which you have experimented with your own color combinations.

With enamel and a small brush you can dress them up with such combinations as yellow with black stripes, ditto with red stripes, orange with black spots, solid yellow, or any shades which strike your fancy. You probably won't come up with anything more generally effective than the red and white, but any one of your gaudy creations may prove more effective on a certain day or in particular waters. With various colors and patterns to select from, you have one more trick up your sleeve when the going's tough.

Whether you use wobblers or spoons, don't be afraid to doctor them up a little whenever they're hard to sell. Hang a tail of fish skin, rubber, or thin pork rind on the trailing hooks and the fluttering action may turn the tide.

Most good pickerel lures are sinkers and, in shallow water, you have little choice but to reel rapidly and steadily to keep the hooks out of the weeds. Such tactics never make for the most strikes, so fish the deeper pickerel grounds as much as possible. Here you can give your lure a much more teasing action without danger of hanging the weeds. Let your spoon settle close to the weeds before starting your retrieve, then raise your rod to the vertical with a single, sharp pump. Lower it immediately, pick up the slack with a few quick turns of the reel, then pump again, continuing the action throughout the retrieve. This keeps your spoon darting ahead, only to fall off as though injured at the completion of each spurt forward. Done to perfection, your retrieve will let the lure settle with a feeble flutter, then snatch it forward and upward just as it seems doomed to sink into the weeds. Pickerel go for that fall-back and you'll get fully as many strikes on the sinking spoon as when it picks up speed.

But tease them as you will, many pickerel will follow your lure all the way to the boat without striking, an annoying habit characteristic of all members of the pike family. Sometimes you can get a strike from a follower by leaving the lure in the water on only a few inches of line and swinging it in a figure eight with the tip of the rod. More often, the fish sees you flourish the rod and the motion spooks him, but you can cross him up with a fast switch:

Have a live minnow hooked and ready in your bait bucket. When you see a pickerel tailing your lure toward the boat, kill the action before he comes close enough to take alarm. He'll sink out of sight and you can bring the spoon in slowly without starting him up again. As quickly as possible, snap the minnow-baited hook to your line in place of the lure, and cast the bait to where you last saw the pickerel. Works like a charm . . . if you have that minnow hooked and waiting.

Trolling

Trolling probably has it over casting wherever pickerel grounds extend well into the lake and you have no need to search out the shoreline pockets. Over large weed beds your chances improve with the amount of water you cover, for you have little to guide you in locating fish. Steady trolling keeps your lure working constantly and, through the law of averages, puts it over more pickerel.

A Dardevle is as deadly trolled as when cast, with the other spoons and wobblers fitting into the trolling picture accordingly. The Dowagiac Spook deserves special mention as a trolling lure, for it seems to need no help from the rod to bring plenty of strikes. With the wobblers you should raise and lower the rod constantly to give them the erratic action which is the key to their effectiveness. They'll bring you biggest returns if you hold to a slow trolling speed but work industriously with the rod.

We can't speak of trolling for pickerel without paying respects to that ancient favorite, the Skinner Fluted Spoon. Though called a "spoon," the lure features a nickel spinner splashed with red which revolves ahead of treble hooks dressed with feathers. It rides closer to the surface than the wobblers and makes a better lure for trolling over weeds which rise fairly close to the surface. Just let it beat its way along and it will provide all the necessary action. This old reliable took pickerel for granddad, and it fools them now as it did then.

Spinning

The spinning rod comes in as handy for taking pickerel on bait as it does in the case of trout or bass. With it you can cast live minnows away from the boat in shallow water and get far more strikes than if you merely lobbed them out with a fly rod. Use a plastic bubble such as the "Buldo" to hold the bait at the correct depth, and cast close to pad patches and other cover close to shore.

Spinning has been especially welcome to the skitterers, for it's the first real answer to their casting needs. Strip baits are too light for the bait-casting rod, too heavy for the fly rod, but shoot out like magic from the spinning reel. This not only makes much lighter work of skittering, but brings more strikes by letting you work from a distance where you won't alarm the fish.

The spinning outfit fills no gap in the casting picture, for the best lures all handle well on the bait-casting rod. You can use small spoons and take pickerel, of course, but your catch will almost always run to smaller fish.

Nevertheless, you may find that your light tackle more than makes up for lack of size in the fish, so you shouldn't rule out the tiny spinning lures without giving them a try.

Fly Fishing

If pickerel feed on insects, they do it so rarely that you can't hope to tempt them with insect imitations. Quite the opposite, however, when you tie on a minnowlike pattern.

Any large bucktail or streamer will take pickerel, but those combining red, white, and/or yellow seem especially attractive. The white or yellow should predominate with the red used as trimming; long white or yellow wings and a collar of bright red hackle, for example.

Few patterns have been designed strictly as pickerel flies, but I know of at least one. H. G. Tapply combined the colors of a popular skittering bait in a creation which he lists in his *The Fly Tyer's Handbook* as merely the "Perch Belly." Here's the dressing, with the author's permission:

Tail: Red and yellow.
Body: Silver, wire ribbed.
Wings: Yellow streamer feathers over white; red topping; junglecock eyes.
Throat: Red.

Whether a pickerel ever mistook it for a perch belly is open to question, but it has all the right colors and brings plenty of strikes.

Use flies tied on long-shank No.-4 (or larger) hooks and stick to the shallow water for your fly fishing. You'll lose few flies to the pickerels' sharp teeth if you go no finer than six-pound test in your leaders, but it pays to call a halt at that point. A spinner ahead of your streamer is a distinct pain in the wrist, but it always means more strikes.

NORTHERN PIKE

Maybe you've heard fishermen speak with disdain of the northern pike. There's no accounting for the tastes of some people—especially those hardheads whose ideas run contrary to our own.

The chief reason for the northern's unpopularity probably lies in his habit of butting his long, ugly snout in where it's not wanted. Trout fishermen look upon pike as a nuisance, and muskie fishermen hold them in even greater contempt. Judged strictly on his own merits, though, the northern pike rates as quite a game fish indeed.

Pike fishing and pickerel fishing are identical up to a point, but where pickerel leave off the pike keep going. You always have a chance of hooking 20-pound fish in pike water, with monsters of twice that weight within the realm of possibility!

Your pickerel techniques will work equally as well on pike, for the two species have almost identical habits. They differ slightly in some respects, however, and a knowledge of these differences helps in pike fishing.

Pike Traits

Pike lurk and pounce just as pickerel do, but they move around more and seem less inclined to bury themselves in the depths of weed jungles. They like weeds, of course, but you'll sometimes find them over rocky bottoms and gravel bars. If the weed beds yield no strikes, go outside them and run your spoon just off the bottom.

In hot weather you may need to go to considerable depth to take pike, for they sometimes move into 40 feet of water of more. Deep trolling with a metal line is always a good midsummer stunt and often the only way to take pike at that time.

The northern's willingness to do without dense cover is evident from the fact that they sometimes thrive in fast-moving streams which have hardly any weed growth. You'll even find them in the fastest currents and in some streams you can catch trout, smallmouths, and northerns from the same run or pool. Ordinarily, though, river pike seek the quiet backwaters where they lurk among the branches of a fallen tree or in the shadow of a boulder. Such retreats are easy to locate and a searching spoon generally stirs up a strike if the stream has a pike population of any significance. River pike holes generally hold several fish, so give each a good working-over.

A small northern will give you the same sort of scrap as a pickerel of the same size, but all resemblance to pickerel fishing ceases when you hook a really large pike. The lunkers have tremendous power in their lithe bodies and unleash it in unexpected bursts which can smash your tackle if you make the mistake of bearing down too hard. Like pickerel, they always seem to have strength for one more dash when you reach out with the net.

Fish Bites Man

Probably something should be said about the danger of badly cut fingers from the wickedly sharp teeth of all the pikes. If you have ever made the sad mistake of reaching into a gaping, fang-studded maw, then you undoubtedly realize that there are *many* things to be said!

A pike's teeth curve inward slightly, and it is almost impossible to reach in among them for a hook without ultimately shedding blood. The fish flops or gasps; one or more teeth prick your fingers and you yank your hand away instinctively. The yanking does the job, producing a nice long cut that's bound to get much worse before it gets better.

Will a pike bite you deliberately, though—clamp right down as though he meant business? Eels and catfish will shut down on a finger when they get the chance, but I always thought that pike sliced you more by accident than by design.

That was my opinion until finally I took liberties with the wrong pike!

Maybe you have never tangled with a pike that would bite you "on purpose," but take my word for it that such critters do exist and don't go looking for one. I've done the pioneer work already, so you stand to prove nothing. Grant me the distinction of discovery like a good sport, and use your pliers to remove all hooks.

Pike Baits

One of the secrets of bait fishing for northerns is to use bait big enough to attract fish of real size. Some fishermen never tumble to this—they use minnows more suitable for bass and pickerel and, in the main, catch only small-to-medium pike. The big fellows, the ones you're after, want something more substantial, so tempt them with bait six to eight inches long.

Suckers are generally available in these sizes and make excellent bait. Golden shiners are even better, but the big ones usually are scarce just when you want them. Fallfish also belong on the preferred list, and these you generally get in the correct size, whenever you're lucky enough to get any at all.

And don't forget yellow perch! These are just as effective on big pike as they are on pickerel.

Pike Lures

The northern's taste in lures coincides almost exactly with the pickerel's. What takes one will take the other, though you should use the larger lures if you want big pike. Here again, you'll have a hard job to find a lure to top the Dardevle. It was a sorry day for the pike tribe when the first one was made.

Fall Fishing

The best time of the year for pike fishing comes in the fall when cooling water puts zip in the big fellows. Then they go on the feed as at no other time, so break out the fishing tackle for a last try on some day when the weather smacks more of hunting than of fishing. Troll your biggest red and white wobbler over the weed beds along their edges. If you use live bait, make it big. Have a man-sized net or gaff handy, and don't settle for anything under ten pounds!

MUSKELLUNGE

The minute you set out to catch a muskie, you're bucking odds that would shame even a bookie. A whole bay may hold only one fish and your chance of finding him in all that water is slim indeed. Even if you're lucky enough to drop your lure where he can see it, it's always a good bet that he won't stir a fin!

Unless you're loaded with luck, nothing counts for so much in muskie fishing as stubborn determination. Getting one of those brag fish is largely a matter of refusing to give up!

Muskie Habits

Tough customer though he is, the muskie has a couple of traits which you can put to good advantage.

The big ones take over certain hunting grounds of their own, and each defends his particular domain against all comers. Next, like all the pike, muskies will often come out of hiding to trail a lure all the way to the boat, even though they have no intentions of hitting it.

Suppose you raise a big fellow who follows but won't take. Discouraging? Far from it! You've come a long way already, for now you know where to find him in the future. One happy day you'll find him in a weak moment, and then he's yours!

Don't write the spot off, either, once you catch your muskie. Another just as big may move right in and make himself at home, so give the place the full treatment your next time out.

Of course, if you're smart, you'll hire a guide and save yourself a lot of wasted effort. He'll know all the likely water and the chances are good that he'll have a few fish marked down for you to work on right off the bat.

If you chance it alone, look for muskies along the edges of shallow bars, in bays and at their mouths, over deep-sunken weed beds, and along shore where weed patches, boulders, and pockets offer cover. Expect to do a lot of casting before you find a fish—if you catch two legal muskies in a solid week of fishing, you've enjoyed better-than-average luck.

Muskies feed mainly on fish, though they snap up ducklings, squirrels, muskrats, and any other birds and small animals who make the mistake of coming within range. Like the cannibals they are, they feed on their own kind and like nothing better for a meal than a northern pike.

Hooked muskies jump more than the other pike, although the real lunkers seldom prove as air-minded as the middleweights. All of them will clean you if you make the mistake of putting too much strain on your tackle during the first hectic minutes of the fray. Keep a taut line, but don't try to stop a muskie until he loses some of his ginger.

Muskie Baits

Just recently a fisherman won a prize with a 49-pound muskie which he caught by using a two and one half-pound smallmouth bass for bait. What's more, he landed the big fish on a fly rod without so much as pricking him with the hook! As you've probably guessed, he was playing the bass when the big muskie rose and gulped it in. Luckily, the fisherman had enough line on his reel to give the fish his head while he swallowed the bass. Some two hours later he brought the muskie to gaff, the victim of careful rod handling and slow strangulation.

This gives you an idea of a big muskie's capacity—this one probably looked on the bass as no more than a snack—but you'll have better luck if you stick to baits of more moderate size. Suckers, six to ten inches long, are the number one bait for muskies, with large minnows and chubs ranking second. Here are a few things to keep in mind if you use either:

Live bait produces best in the fall when muskies are on the feed.

Cast your bait or troll it. Either method is better than still-fishing, unless you have a particular fish to work on.

If you *have* spotted a muskie's hangout, then that's the time to let your sucker or minnow swim in one place.

Give slack whenever you get a strike on live bait, wait while the muskie swallows it, then set the hook hard when he starts to move off.

Use wire leaders at least ten inches long.

Bait Casting

Day-in and day-out, your best bet for muskies is a stiff, rugged casting rod and an assortment of proven muskie lures.

Remember that muskie fishing is largely a case of licking the law of averages. You build up your chances by covering as much water as possible and trying the various depths. Play the percentages with some such program as this:

First, work the shallow weed beds thoroughly with your surface splutterers. If this fails to bring a strike, move to the middle depths and offer them a diving plug or a spinner and bucktail. Next, try a deep-running wobbler along the outer edges of the weed beds.

If you raise a follower, swing your lure through a figure eight if he trails it all the way to the boat; this may coax him into banging it!

If he proves stubborn, here's a tip to remember: More big muskies than you'll ever see have been marked down, then caught through no trick but steady casting, maybe for as long as a solid hour. Stick with any muskie you locate; pester him with a plug until he can't stand the sight of it!

A few final bait casting tips:

Fill your reel with rugged line—24-pound test is none too heavy.

Use wire bait-casting leaders to avoid a tooth-cut line.

When you get a strike, hit your fish hard, hit him again, then sock it to him once more for luck. You've raised him, now make sure he stays stuck!

Trolling

Trolling has it over bait casting when hot weather sends the muskies into deep water. Use a metal line or heavy sinker to hold your lure near bottom and troll at a fairly fast clip. Any of your sinking or diving lures will serve for trolling, but a Dardevle trolled and "worked" at the same time makes a strong bid for top honors.

If you have no luck with artificials, try a live sucker. Troll very slowly or drift, so the sucker swims naturally a few feet above bottom.

Tricky, unpredictable business, this muskie fishing, but when all's said and done, you'll make out best if you follow these two rules:

Hire a good guide.
Keep plugging!

8. Panfish

WHO NEEDS ANY TRICKS UP HIS SLEEVE TO CATCH panfish? Why, the little cusses bite on almost anything, any time.

That's an opinion shared by many fishermen . . . until they deliberately set out to catch a mess. Then they find that panfish don't always come as easily as they thought!

YELLOW PERCH

You caught them by the dozens early last spring? They had just spawned then and were so hungry they'd grab anything you threw out. But how about that time in July when you went out to "catch enough for a meal" . . . and got skunked?

You just didn't happen to strike a school? Bet you had more than one school under your boat and didn't know it. Bet, too, that with a few simple tricks you could have caught what you needed to eat, even though you bothered to carry no bait but that can of worms.

First Trick

Take that sinker off your line, make as long casts as you can handily, and let your bait drift slowly to the bottom as any worm would when sinking of its own accord. Almost every fish that swims—bottom feeders excluded—will snap up a slowly sinking bait at times when they won't touch one pulled down rapidly by a chunk of lead. Even minnows are suspicious of sinkers, as you can prove to your own satisfaction the next time you try to catch some for bait.

Second Trick

Maybe they don't feel in the mood for a whole worm, so nip off a small dab and try it on a No.-14 hook. You'll need a split shot to take this down, and this leads to a trick within a trick: Pinch the shot to the shank of the hook just back of the eye, instead of to the leader as you normally would. The shot gives your hook a nymphlike appearance and the bit of worm advertises it as something good to eat. Jig it ever so lightly to complete the deception.

Three worm rigs for perch

Third Trick

Tie a small spinner ahead of your bait and troll very slowly, or cast it with your spinning rod if you have it along. The secret of using a spinner-worm combination for perch is to move the lure fast enough to attract fish, then slack off for a moment or two. Perch may trail the spinner without taking the worm, but they'll generally dart in and grab it as soon as you kill the action.

They are easy stunts, but with them you can take perch when plain dangle-fishing won't get you a smell!

Baits

Worms came in for first mention, not because they top the list of perch baits, but because they're easy to get and come in for the most use. The best bait? Minnows, across the board. Little two-inchers are tops, but those an inch longer will do almost as well.

Attractive as these tiny minnows are, you can gum the works by fishing them more dead than alive. To serve them up fresh and lively, use small hooks—8's or 10's—of fine, light wire such as are used for tying dry flies. These injure the minnows but little and they stay pert and full of life. Makes a world of difference!

Ordinarily, you need only still-fish with small minnows to catch plenty of perch, but there come times when you have to go one step farther. Hang one of the same small minnows on two No.-10 hooks tied in tandem to a nylon snell, and troll it behind a spinner. Something of a bother to rig those little baits, but perch will dive for them on days when they turn their noses up at everything else.

If you can't get minnows, try the smallest crawfish you can find, or undersized hellgrammites. These, along with any grubs you can lay hand to, often have it over worms when the perch turn finicky.

But so much for plain catching perch; let's turn to big perch, those fat, hump-backed fellows that weigh nearly a pound. They travel in schools and wherever you catch one, you generally find more waiting. Let's go find us one of those schools.

Tie a swivel to your leader, snap on a fly-rod Flatfish and start trolling. Add enough sinker to take the lure within a few feet of the bottom, but not enough to keep you hung up. You'll take perch—that little Flatfish murders them—but keep moving until a big one whangs it. Then over with the anchor, and down at them with some lively minnows. The chances are good that you'll have other hefty perch beneath you, ready to give you some of the liveliest fishing you've had in a long time. Much better to hunt those lurkers down than to wait for them to come to you.

Even though you don't strike a school of big ones on the first try, you'll discover a first-class perch lure in the Flatfish. Another to match it is the small red and white fly-rod wobbler. Wherever there are perch, you won't have to drag either of these lures far to get results.

If you decide that trolling is something you'd like to do more of and often, it's then best to rig up a rod for this special purpose. This is easily done by splicing about 30 feet of light metal line to an ordinary bait-casting line and spooling this combination on a fly reel. This long metal "leader" will take your small lures down to the perch, but will impose no strain that a fly rod can't shrug off. Makes a far more satisfactory trolling rig than you get by adding a hefty sinker, and its use is not by any means confined to the taking of perch. Such an outfit has its place in trolling for bass, pike, trout, and other fish when you want to go to moderate depths with light lures and use light tackle.

While on the subject of big perch, it is worth pointing out for the benefit of those unacquainted with these hefty fellows, that their taking bears no resemblance to dragging in the little chaps eight or nine inches long. They give you a smart tussle, and, on a stringer, look more impressive than the same number of medium-sized bass. Such bass are merely bass, but in taking a string of perch in the 12-to-15-inch bracket you gain the satisfaction that goes with the catching of real lunkers of any species.

It would be especially nice if such obligingly abundant fish as yellow perch would give you fly-fishing sport, but they don't. They won't come to dry flies worth a hoot, and taking them on wet flies and streamers is anything but exciting. You must wait for your fly to settle after each cast, then fish it very slowly if you are to get strikes. This wouldn't be so bad if they would haul off and sock it, but perch seldom do. If they hit at all, it's more of a nip or a bunt than an honest-to-goodness strike.

So, as far as fly fishing for perch is concerned, there's just one trick worth remembering: Bait your fly with a worm!

SUCKERS ON THE WET FLY!

There! This heading should show that I'm all for fly fishing whenever it's the least bit practical. And fly fishing for suckers is the least practical thing I can think of.

But we're going right ahead with this thing, now that we're into it, for you *can* take suckers on a wet fly.

As a kid, I used to fish for big, golden fellows that sometimes went as heavy as four pounds. Although worms were the accepted bait, they didn't bring bites fast enough to suit me; and this set me looking for some way to speed things up.

Watching the deep, quiet pools for possible clues, I finally noticed that any light-colored patch on bottom attracted each sucker that came along—every last one of them would drift toward a white stone, for instance, and give it a nosing over. Struck by sudden inspiration, I ripped a strip from my white handkerchief, hung it on my hook and plunked it into the pool accompanied by a heavy sinker. Sure enough, the nearest sucker, one of the biggest, promptly dipped down to test the white rag with his rubbery snout, and I as promptly whanged the hook into him with a heave of my long cane pole.

From then on I did my sucker fishing with a bit of white cloth, though always in private, for I had no intention of sharing my hard-won secret. In pools where I couldn't see my "lure" on bottom, I'd count to 20 and heave. Even this hit-or-miss technique brought twice as many suckers as worms ever had.

So, substitute a large, white streamer for the rag, sink it with a goodly chunk of lead, and you can take suckers on a fly as advertised.

BLUEGILLS

Want some fun? Toss your lightest fly rod and a box of dry flies in the car and head for the nearest bluegill water. Go at it right, and you'll have them fighting for your floaters.

Topnotch sport any time, but particularly soothing to the ego if the trout have just finished making you look like a dub!

I know a fellow who has bluegills almost in his back yard, and he loves to show them off.

"Fish till you catch five," he'll tell you when he gets you in his boat. "Then it's my turn."

You settle down for some pleasant casting, only to find yourself taking the oars before you've hardly started. Things continue at this merry pace until you conclude that bluegills just sit up and beg to be caught.

Wrong! You've had fast and furious fishing largely because you're out with a fellow who knows his bluegills and all the little tricks that bring them up.

First, take a look at the flies he brought along for both of you to use. No particular patterns, but notice that all are bushy, heavily hackled jobs—some bivisibles, others with deer-hair wings, and a few minature deer-hair bass bugs—whiskery, bulky flies that ride high on the water and look like buggy mouthfuls. These flies on No.-8 or -10 hooks will get you many more strikes than the small, delicate flies which fool trout. Important bluegill know-how!

"Twitch it a little," he said, after your fly had rested on the water a moment. You did—skated the spidery fly a few inches—and were fast to a fish! Simple, but would *you* have thought of it? Bet you'd have let that fly stay there motionless out of respect for your trout-fishing experience. You know better now, though—little twitches take big bluegills.

Then, too, your partner saw to it that you fished at the right time and in the most likely places. Made you wait until late afternoon to go out and, even then, picked a sheltered cove where you could fish a shaded shore with no wind

Conditions for good bluegill fishing

to ruffle the water. Late afternoon and evening hours, calm water, and shade—three important factors that you could have overlooked.

Finally, he coached you well. "See this or that little opening in the pads or weeds?" he was continually saying. "Why'n't you take a poke at it, long's we're here." Eventually it dawned on you that you were taking most of your fish from those small pockets you would have passed up. Then you lengthened line and started shooting for them without being told. Pinpoint casting, bigger fish, more of them—a big improvement any way you looked at it.

The whole works in one easy lesson, but don't forget that it would have taken you a lot longer to dope it out by yourself!

It seems almost a shame to speak of anything but dry flies in connection with bluegills, for they give you such a whale of a good time when they'll rise. Sometimes, though, it's too windy, too cold, or too bright, and then you have no choice but to turn to wet flies or bait. If you tie on a wet fly, here are a few hints which should help:

Pick a dull-colored pattern like the Quill Gordon, instead of the gay numbers usually recommended for panfish. Bright flies will bring strikes, but see if you don't get more by imitating natural nymphs and insects.

Split a few No.-6 shot and space them along your leader to take your fly down quickly and help hold it where it belongs.

Retrieve very slowly with the lightest of twitches to sell the idea that the fly is an actual insect.

If a bare fly brings no strikes, try adding just enough worm to cover the barb of the hook.

As a last resort, say good-by to casting ease and tie a small spinner ahead of the fly.

If you use bait, try catalpa worms if you can get them, for they make a particularly killing bait for bluegills. Cut in small pieces and fish on No.-10 hooks.

Worms, grubs, crickets, corn borers, and almost any insect or larva you can name will take bluegills. Keep your baits and hooks small.

Here's a little-used trick: Bait a No.-10 wet fly with half a worm and fish it not as a fly, but as bait. The combination often wins you more bites than a worm on a plain hook.

Dress up your hooks with luminous paint, or use the "gold"-plated variety. Bait with a small piece of worm and jig often to make the hook twinkle.

To call them around you and keep them stirred up, try this: Fill a pocket, with crumbled shale or pieces of broken-up clam shells. To get action, flick bits of shale or shell into the water one at a time. The flat pieces flutter and sparkle on their way to the bottom and fish go crazy trying to investigate first this one and that. Excited and bite-minded, they're pushovers for a lightly jigged bait.

Along the edges of quiet bayous and rivers in the sunny South, where bluegills are known as "brim," the drooping branches of overhanging trees are often loaded with all sorts of insect life. This gives you your chance to do a little impromptu "chumming"; move in quietly, flail all the foliage within reach with your paddle or oar, then back off an easy casting distance. Nearby bluegills, and maybe a bass or two, will close in to feed on the insects that you so rudely awakened and knocked to the water. Cash in on this induced feeding by dropping a dry fly or small bass bug in the midst of the activity.

In the same Southern waters floating mats of grass are common sights, and these let you get in more telling licks of the paddle. Ease your boat up to the edge of the mat, then reach out with the paddle and paw a hole in the grass two or three feet in diameter. This done, pound all the surrounding grass vigorously with the flat of the blade. This knocks loose the grass shrimp and other assorted creatures hiding in the mat, and sends them drifting toward bottom. A small wet fly or artificial nymph, weighted with a split shot and jigged through the open hole you took pains to prepare, should take its toll from among the excited brim that gather to snap up the sinking insects.

CRAPPIES AND CALICOES

I had hoped to give you some positive means of identifying these near-twins, but I didn't get anywhere. Under the heading "Distinguishing Characteristics," my reference makes this airtight distinction: *Calicoes have seven or more dorsal spines; crappies have seven or less.*

Actually, you generally can tell them apart easily enough, for the black markings on the calicoes are much more pronounced than those on the crappies, leading to the more descriptive names of "black crappie" for the calico, and "white crappie" for his close relative. When it comes to catching them, we can lump the two species together as "crappies," for to all of our intents and purposes they have identical habits.

The crappie's big mouth pegs him as a minnow feeder. He'll gobble an occasional worm, cricket, or grasshopper, but his interest centers largely in small fish. Meat-minded, he shows little or no interest in dry flies, but he'll give you plenty of light-tackle sport under the surface.

Hottest tip of all: Use your spinning rod! Tiny spoons, spinners, and wobblers are positively deadly on crappies. Part of their effectiveness lies in their natural attraction for these fish, but fully as much comes from the distance you can get with these small metal lures. You'll find that unlike bluegills, who hang pretty much to shoreline cover, crappies often school in open water where you have no hints to their whereabouts. Covering the water with long casts of the spinning rod is one of the quickest ways to find a school. Work the lure deep, keep it darting and fluttering, and you'll soon have them coming.

Another tip for lively crappie fishing: Troll with your fly rod. Hang a red and white fly-rod wobbler on your leader, troll slowly, and work the wobbler with the rod to give it an erratic action. If you don't have a fly-rod lure with you, cut a minature skittering bait from the first fish you catch—a narrow, two-inch slice—and troll with this, adding enough sinker to hold it well down. You can skitter this bait and take crappies, too, for they love that fish taste!

Although crappies seldom offer at a dry fly, they go for streamers. Here are a few fly-fishing hints:

Find a school by trolling, then switch to flies after you have fish located. Much faster than starting from scratch with blind casting.

Try small streamers, but change to bigger ones—2's and 4's—if the little ones let you down. Crappies have those big mouths for a purpose!

Use and ungreased silk line, preferably an old one that will absorb water and sink quickly. Waiting long moments for your line to sink after each cast is irksome business.

Hurry your fly down with a few tiny shot or bits of lead spaced along the leader.

Vary your retrieves. Sometimes a slow, halting action turns the trick, while other times a fast-moving fly brings more strikes. Remember that crappies are minnow-catches and accustomed to snatching their food on the fly.

Never give up on flies before adding a spinner. Of all the panfish, crappies fall hardest for a spinner-fly combination.

When it comes to natural baits, nothing can hold a candle to two-inch minnows. Use small, light-wire hooks to keep your minnows smart and lively. Although crappies have large mouths, they may turn the bait before swallowing it, so it's usually best to pause a moment or two before setting the hook. Handle hooked crappies carefully, for the flesh of their mouths is tender.

BULLHEADS

Bullheads may look stupid, but you won't fool them with any of your fancy didoes and fake baits. They'll settle only for something good to eat. For a fish, that's showing pretty good judgment!

Probably, though, it's just because they have better tasters and smellers than most other fiish, They can smell out food in short order and, if you want to draw them together, try this:

Have your butcher save a box of bones for you. Wire them together or put them in a burlap bag, then sink them where you intend to fish. Go back the next few nights, and you're likely to find the bullheads holding a regular camp meeting.

Bullheads usually bite best at night, but don't hesitate to go out on a rainy day if you hanker for a fish fry. Sometimes they bite as well then as after dark.

Here's a switch that will often get you bigger bullheads: Instead of the usual worms, use whole, dead minnows—the "deader" the better—or chunks of larger fish. These baits send out a rich perfume which brings the big ones in on the beam. Pieces of meat on the "ripe" side will call them, too, but fish seems to do the job better.

Whatever you fish with, lay it smack on bottom and leave it there—they'll find it. Use big hooks, too, for bullheads aren't squeamish with a bait and generally swallow small hooks so deeply that you have a tough job getting them out.

That's about all there is to catching bullheads: just pick up your rod and go. Does you good to leave all your fancy doodads home once in a while.

JUST FISH

Sometimes I think we let a species' reputation or social standing play much too big a role in deciding whether we should have fun catching its members. Game fish? Yes! Panfish? Well, maybe. "Rough" fish? Not so you'd notice it! But they're all fish, all have fins and a tail, and all will give at least some measure of sport to the fellow who gets down from his high horse to clinch with them.

If you think differently, I wish you could come with me some time to Lake Champlain where you can dangle a minnow or hightcrawler and expect any one of 12 or 15 different kinds of fish to be the next to grab it. The line picks up and starts out slowly and you "let him have it" for a few moments. Then you set the hook and something whumps the rod down against the gunwale hard before you can release the reel. The line races out as the fish makes a powerful run—is it a whopper of a bass, a big northern, or is it a ling, a hefty sheepshead, or a big, old catfish set? If you can't tell, *then what difference does it make?*

One of the biggest kicks I ever got while fishing came the morning when my wife hooked something we never once saw (to recognize) for at least 20 minutes of hectic battle. We had anchored in a shallow, weedy bay at the mouth of a creek. Shortly thereafter I noticed schools of golden shiners passing under the boat, so I rigged a small hook and caught some for the minnow bucket. (Good business anywhere, incidentally, to catch your bait on the scene if you can. The "native" bait usually brings better results than an imported variety.)

A few minutes later three bobbers floated near the boat—my wife's, our youngster's, and my own—and each held a deep-bellied golden shiner just above the tops of the weeds. The three floats went unmolested for only a few minutes, then: Kerchug! One of the bright-colored bobber—my wife's—went under with such suddenness and force that it sent a miniature geyser two feet in the air. The slack line my wife had coiled in the bottom of the boat went snaking out through the guides of her fly rod, the fish finally stopping just before coming against the reel.

"Let him chew on it," I advised. Then, a minute or two later, "Tighten up, now, and sock it to him."

She did—jabbed it to him good on a tight line. Krrrr, went the reel, and it kept going. No leaps from the fish, no turns, no nothing; just a steady course straight down the bay and no stopping. I saw the backing start through the guides and prayed that it would outlast the run.

Whether or not it would have, I'll never know, for the line suddenly went slack. The fish was gone—just like that.

That fish, whatever it was, must have been as long as a pulp log, I told myself, and the thought made me anything but happy over its loss. Worst of all, I could find no honest way of pinning the blame on my wife. She had committed no error, which is just like a woman. If only I could have pointed and accusing finger and yelled, "I told you so!" I would have felt much better about the whole thing.

As it was, I could do nothing but hold my tongue and hang on another shiner, glumly reflecting the while that we stood little chance of hooking another such critter. I was dead wrong, however; the fresh shiner had no more than sunk when the bobber went under every bit as violently as it had before.

At the sting of the hook, this fish took up exactly where the other had left off. The reel chattered and again we were treated to a show of backing. This time the hook held fast, and finally the fish turned and headed back toward the boat. But he soon was off an another long run, and another and another thereafter. There was no stopping him with a fly rod; the only thing that kept him from cleaning the reel, in fact, was his failure to continue in one direction for that one added moment that would have taken the last foot of line. Snubbed tight, he would have broken the ten-pound nylon leader like so much thread.

Already we had lost one monster before we could identify it. The thought that this could happen a second time seemed almost too much to bear; yet, as the battle went on and on, this seemed all too likely for comfort. Once, when the fish cut under the bow of the boat and I leaned out to clear the line, I glimpsed a great, dark shape plowing through the weeds, but that was all. We never knew until the very last what manner of creature was putting up that terrific struggle; and the fear that we would lose it before we did know just about doubled the excitement. Playing a fish that had been seen and recognized, no matter how large, holds no comparable thrill. This was no big pike, no huge bass—no, indeed. This was a big what-the-devil-is-it who at any moment might decide to attack the boat!

What matter, then, that our "prize" finally turned out to be a great bowfin with ugly, flattened head, wide mouth spiked with wicked teeth, and two of the meanest-looking little eyes that you ever could gaze into? He had handed my wife a battle that left her exhausted, and had given the three of us 20 bug-eyed minutes during which our hearts had never once left our throats.

And the other big devil that broke away? He *could* have been a muskie, the biggest northern pike in the lake—anything. That's the fun of fishing "just for fish"—you never know what will happen, and sometimes you don't know what did!

9. Ice Fishing

WITH ALL DUE RESPECT FOR PSYCHOLOGISTS AND their complicated ways of testing a man's sanity, they have overlooked a simple method which they could apply in all our Northern states. Merely pick a blustery midwinter day when the mercury hovers around zero and make a tally of all those who refuse to stick their noses outside warm, steam-heated homes. Then run a count on those who are pounding holes in the ice of wind-swept lakes and dipping bare hands in icy minnow buckets. Deciding which group lacks the sound, sober judgment that goes with sanity shouldn't be very hard.

Tools of the Trade

Holding the subject of tackle in reserve, the following items of basic equipment will meet most ice-fishing needs: Spud, long-handled skimmer, minnow bucket, and, of course, plenty of warm clothing. None but the spud warrants further comment.

Any old spud won't do . . . not when the ice has built up to a foot and a half in thickness. Then you need a heavy spud with a narrow blade—one which comes down with authority and bites deeply with each stroke. The edge should be beveled on only one side to throw chips toward the center of the hole as you work. Keep the edge sharp and free from nicks with a stone, and be sure to tie a loop of rawhide or rope to the top. Slip the loop over your wrist while cutting to avoid losing the spud through the hole.

When it comes to actual tackle you have a hundred-and-one choices, depending on how you fish and for what. Let's take them up as they apply to the various species and methods.

Pike and Pickerel

The cold water of winter doesn't affect the feeding habits of members of the pike family. You'll find them lurking in weed beds and preying on lesser fish, as they do during the summer monts. Just go after them with a bucket of minnows.

Tilts

Considerable ingenuity has gone into designing tilts or tip-ups, but there are really only two types with significant differences. One holds part of the line above the ice, while the other operates with all the line in the water. The underwater job cannot freeze in, for all the reserve line is on a spool which juts into the water when the tilt is set. A slender rod set in a tube of hard grease springs the flag the instant a bite turns the spool, no matter if the hole is completely iced over. This

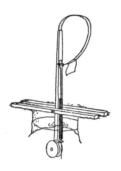

Underwater reel tip-up

Top-water reel (below) and
detail of reel (above)

gives you a free-running line in the coldest weather, and often means the difference between a fish and a stolen bait.

If you use top-water tilts, keep the holes well skimmed and keep reserve line on spools where it will pay out readily. You can buy spools ready-made, or make acceptable substitutes from those which typewriter ribbons come wound on. Lacking either, get a strip of quarter-inch pine two inches wide and cut it in five-inch lengths. Scallop the ends of each piece and drill holes from edge to edge at the midpoints. Place washers on either side, shove flat-headed nails through the holes and drive them into the edges of the tilts. Wind your lines on these holders and they'll spin as readily as spools when pike grab your minnows and head off with them.

About 40 feet of line on each spool will give all you need for pike and pickerel. Use coarse line that you can handle with numb fingers. For tooth-proof leaders, use foot-long strands of go-pound nylon. Tie on hooks to match the size of your bait and finish with a single buckshot above each leader. Carry extra sinkers with you for any jumbo baits you may use.

Setting in

Admittedly, you don't have much to go on in choosing precise locations for your tilts. You'll make sure you're over pike or pickerel grounds, of course, but the ice gives you no helpful hints as to exactly where fish may lie. Nevertheless, you can use a certain amount of craftiness in planning your layout. Space most of your tilts over water which varies in depth from about five feet to ten or 12—don't fish at one depth only. Save out a few tilts for "prospecting." Go near shore and set a couple where the water is only two or three feet deep, then stick in another pair at the outer edge of the weeds in 15 or 20 feet of water.

If one of your outlying tilts goes up it may signal a lucky hit from a straggler, or it may mean that fish are using the shallow water near shore or the outside depths. If you get another strike, start moving your concentration of lines in the indicated direction. With a few widely dispersed tilts you can sometimes trail down the good spots that you would fail to find otherwise.

Judging from the holes some fishermen cut, they expect to hook something the size of a tuna. Draw a 12-inch circle on paper, then try to picture a fish too large to come through a hole that size. Big holes mean unnecessary work and possible all-over duckings, so practice reasonable economy. Just make sure that the bottom edges are trimmed of all spurs so fish can slip through easily.

When you have a hole skimmed and ready, test the depth with a sounding weight, then adjust the line to hold the bait about 18 inches above the bottom when the tilt is set. Loop your line to the trigger with a slip knot which unties with a pull—you won't feel like picking at knots when you wind up after sundown.

Bait the hook with a lively minnow and put him to work, but check on a couple of points before you leave. If you're using top-water tilts, does the line enter the center of the hole, or at the edge where it will freeze to the ice quickly? And is the tilt in working order? Better to test it now than to find out later that a stuck flag has robbed you of a fish.

Dull-day Tactics

If flags start popping as soon as you have your lines set in, fine and dandy. It doesn't always work that way, though, and you may need to tease them a little. Try these stunts:

Make a quick trip over your tilts, raising your minnows a few feet and dropping them back. Quite often you'll have a flag up before you complete the circuit. If not, go around again, and this time draw each minnow up about three feet, tie a loop in the line, and let the bait hang at the new level. As soon as you have finished, let the minnows back down gain in the same order that you pulled them up .This some-times works wonders, probably because the pike or pickerel "reason" that if those minnows are going to act that crazily, they'd better snap them up while they still have the chance.

Try dropping a handful of dry oatmeal or corn meal down each hole. This chums small fish under the holes and they in turn attract pike.

Or, if you have a jigging spoon, raise the minnow in each hole and jig vigorously a few minutes. Even if you don't get a whack on the jig, you may toll a pike in and he'll take your minnow when you drop it back down.

Old-timers sometimes thread large pearl buttons above the sinkers or tie on thin streamers of red or white cloth. These act as attractors when towed around by lively minnows.

Hang two minnows on the same hook. This trick tempts pike and pickerel in the winter as well as in the summer.

In any event, don't just sit back and wait for action. Advertise your wares like any good huckster—you'll take more fish and fewer ice clinkers will from in the blood stream.

I am not, however, trying to sell you the idea that you can never get skunked. Even though water temperatures and water conditions must remain pretty constant under the ice, there are days when, for reasons known only to themselves, the fish refuse to feed. No amount of teasing will win bites during the worst of these dry spells, and this you should remember before writing off a new pond or lake as worthless on the strength of your first try. The picture can change completely overnight—maybe the next day you could have cleaned up using the very same holes.

All I know is that the winter feeding habits of fish are as unpredictable and variable as are these traits in warm weather. They'll sulk one day, hit the next, and you never know until you pound those holes.

Pickerel and Pike Baits

Use the same small fish that make good summertime baits. Suckers four to six inches long are among the best, for they have the most life on the hook. Shiners, golden shiners, dace, chubs and all other members of the minnow family bring good results. Try to get them in the four-inch-or-better sizes. Don't forget that pike and pickerel feed regularly on small perch. Jig a few if you can and bait some of your tilts with them. (Another trick for a dull day, and a good one!)

When fishing for northerns, bait a couple of tilts with really big suckers as a come-on for whoppers. Foot-long baits are quite in order, though you'll need to tighten the action of your tilts to keep these big suckers from springing the flags. You can do this by holding the flag down with fine thread that will part easily, or with a rubber band. A pair of big baits lend spice to your fishing, for you know that if one of those tied-down flags springs, something's doing and no fooling!

Tending and Hauling

Dyed-in-the-wool ice fishermen will tell you that you can have your rises to a dry fly or bass bug—give them a sprung flag waving jauntily in the winter breeze. No question about it, the big thrill comes when a flag flies up and lets you know that something's cooking down there under the ice. Go to it on the double—that's part of the fun—but take your time once you get there. Let pike and pickerel move off with the bait; they generally take slack slowly and almost never strip the spool bare before stopping. Give them a minute or two to gorge an ordinary bait, and four or five if using big suckers. Take up slack gently until you can feel the fish, then yank the hook into him hard.

Take it easy with hooked fish, for you have no springy rod to take up shock. Give a big pike his head until he tires, never trying to bring him through the hole while he's still fresh. Have a gaff in your kit when fishing for northerns and always use it to land heavy fish. If you try to heave them out by the line the hook may rip loose and leave you with nothing but regrets.

Jigging

Pike jigs are generally light metal lures designed to dart and zoom when dropped on a slack line, most strikes coming while the jig flutters downward. Jigging to attract pike to your minnows has already been mentioned, but the method is a fish-taker in its own right. There's just one big secret to jigging pike and pickerel: Do your jigging on Mondays!

Superstition? Not by a long shot! On Monday you can jig in all those vacant holes left by Sunday's horde of fishermen. March up one line of holes and down the nest, jigging for only a few moments in each. This gives you the chance to cover almost as much water as thought bait casting, and you'll pick up a tidy number of pike—big perch, too—if you keep moving. A dab of meat on the jig hook helps. Use a minnow tail, perch eye, or shred of skin, just enough to lend taste appeal but too little to hinder the darting action.

Walleyes

The walleyed "pike" belongs to the perch family and hasn't the remotest connection with the pike tribe, a fact which is perfectly apparent from his appearance. Walleyes travel in schools—a perch trait—and their winter wanderings follow the same general course from one season to the next, winding up late in the winter near spawning grounds. Local fishermen always know when to expect walleyes over this reef or the other, and when they will enter certain bays. Take your cue from them when fishing large lakes where walleyes have plenty of room to roam.

Here are a few more ways in which walleyes differ from true pike:

They don't lurk in the weeds. Walleye grounds depend upon the seasonal migrations rather than upon the character of the bottom.

They school in the greatest numbers in late winter, moving into fairly shallow water and following the shoreline as they work slowly toward the spawning grounds. Late-season fishing is therefore the best, provided you have inside information on the runs.

Walleyes hang close to the bottom. Raise your baits no more than six inches whenever the bottom is clean.

Although they can swallow fairly large fish if they have to, walleyes seem to prefer the little fellows. Three-inchers make the best bait, with shiners ranking first among the minnows.

Compared to pike, walleyes bite very gently. They are master bait stealers and often work you for a free minnow without springing the tilt. For this, and other good reasons, you'll take more walleyes if you leave your tilts at home and fish with a line of "whips."

Walleye "Whips"

Cut slender hardwood saplings at least six feet long and trim all the way to their thin, pliant tips. Spud slanting holes for the butts, pack with slush, then prop the whips in forked sticks so the tips lean over the fishing holes. Test the depth and tie the correct length of line to each tip, leaving a little extra to wind down the whip and tie at the base just for safety's sake. Tie on your hooks—No.-4 is a good size—and pinch a two-ounce sinker to each line. Now you're ready to bait up.

In the whips you have the sensitive rigs you need for walleyes, for the slender saplings will dip at the slightest nibble. Even more important, you now have the means of luring fish in for the kill through action made possible by the springy whips and heavy sinkers. Walk along your lines—they should be about six feet apart—pulling each whip down a couple of feet and releasing it quickly. The released sapling sweeps upward, the big sinker pulls it back, it lifts again, and so on. A quick once-over, and you set your whole line of minnows to dancing and shimmering. The flash and motion will call walleyes like magic and you're in for fast action when a school closes in on your closely spaced lines.

Have a care how you handle hooked walleyes for they have extremely tender mouths. Haul them smoothly, but speed up gradually as they near the hole. In this way they come out of the water largely under their own momenturn, and you avoid that last-minute heave which so often tears the hook free.

Perch

Yellow perch are the prime favorites of legions of ice fishermen, and small wonder. Almost always (but not quite) you can count on perch to give you action, while a line of pike tilts may not flip a flag for hours on end. Moreover, perch are as fine eating as their cousins, the walleyes, especially when icy water has made their flesh firm and flavorsome.

Perch Baits

Maybe you've heard that to catch perch through the ice, you need only to find a school. Don't believe it. Shanty fishermen often decoy (more of this later) big schools of perch to their lines, only to have them refuse to bite until the fishermen hit on the right bait through trial and error. Perch can be as finicky as the next fish, so carry a variety of baits and keep changing until you find the one that works best.

Perch feed on small fish, so minnows make one of the most reliable baits. You need tiny two-inchers that the perch can swallow at a gulp after bunting them a few times.

A single perch eye makes one of the best jigging baits, whenever perch are in the mood to take it. Sometimes they are, and sometimes they aren't; you can only tell by trying. If eyes go begging, try jigging with the tail-half of a minnow.

Worms are always a good bet, for they come as a treat in midwinter. Sometimes a small piece works better than the whole article. Look for worms in dirt cellars, under manure piles, and over buried steam pipes. Better yet, get permission to dig at a commercial greenhouse.

Any and all grubs will take perch. Poke for them in rotted stumps and under the bark of dead trees. Goldenrod galls—the hard bulbs which form on the stalks—contain tiny grubs which perch like. Carry the galls with you and cut them open as you need bait.

Perch Methods

Tip-ups make about the poorest rigs for perch fishing, for you can run yourself ragged tending flags yet wind up with but very few fish. In the winter you must often go to depths of 50 feet or more to find perch, and this means that you must use heavy sinkers or fuss and fiddle endlessly to work your lines down through the holes. Then, when a perch springs the tilt, the released lead tumbles past his nose, tugs sharply at his jaw, and he drops the bait in alarm. Rig the sinker below the bait and it works no better—it pulls at the fish as soon as he trips the tilt.

One of the big secrets of deep-water perch fishing is to use a setup which will yield to their light bites and, at the same time, will hold a heavy sinker above them where they won't feel its weight. Large corks or bobbers do this to perfection whenever you fish with only two or three lines and can watch them closely. Use corks which barely float under the pull of the sinker and you'll miss few bites if you set the hook the instant the cork dips under.

If you want to spread more lines around, small whips will serve better than the bobbers, for you can see them farther. Cut thin, green two-foot shoots and lean them over the holes as you do the bigger walleye whips. They'll twitch at the lightest tug and their limber action will result in as many hooked perch as do the bobbers. If you have tip-ups whose flags are attached to ribbons of spring steel you can use these as whips by leaving them unset and tying your lines to the rings at the flag ends. The sinkers draw them down in curves and the flags will jiggle with each bite.

The slickest perch whips I have ever used were made from two-foot sections of a broken bandsaw blade. The teeth were ground off, loops of wire soldered to the ends for line holders, and the opposite ends seated in ten-inch lengths of broom handle by shoving in sawed slits and wrapping with electrician's tape. The steel blades are so limber that perch take the minnows without suspecting that they're tied to anything . . . exactly the way it should be!

But the boys who make it rough on perch—the real specialists—will tell you phooey on your bobbers, whips, and tilts. They'll be right, too, if you don't care how hard you work for your fish.

These fellows set out with a spud, minnows, a single jigging line, and a gunny sack, for they intend to catch perch and no fooling. On their jig sticks they have 25 yards of G level line in the best oil finish. The line sports a two-ounce sinker, a short nylon leader, and a No.-8 hook. They whang a small hole through the ice, kick out only the largest chips, then drop the big sinker through the remaining slush.

With the bait a foot or two off bottom, they jig their minnow, minnow tail, or perch eye with a motion so slight that it amounts to hardly more than a tremble. If nothing happens in the first few minutes—and this is the top secret of jigging perch—they haul in and move to a new spot. Sooner or later they drop their bait into a school of feeding perch and the gunny sack then takes on weight rapidly. The bait hardly reaches bottom when a perch has it and is on his way to the top. In a matter of seconds the rebaited hook is on its way down again as the loose coils of smooth line slither rapidly into the hole after the big sinker.

Perch fishing is a matter of making hay while the sun shines—catching as many as possible before you lose the school—so you should use eyes whenever the perch will take them. With these you lose no time in rebaiting, as a single eye will account for many perch. You simply flip one fish off the hook, and you're after another before you can say scat. Incidentally, you needn't worry that you'll not feel bites in spite of the heavy sinker. Its weight is constant, and the slightest additional pull registers as plainly as though you had no sinker at all.

There's a trick to hooking perch that some ice fishermen never get the hang of. They can't make up their minds to yank, and are forever waiting for each perch to "bite just a little harder." He never does, so he generally escapes with a whole hide. Set the hook the instant the bobber pops under, the whip twitches, or you feel a nibble on your jig line. Indecision costs you perch, as does any attempt to wait them out.

One of the best ways to hook perch while jigging is to "snatch-hook" them without waiting to feel a bite at all. You merely lower your jig line and work it several times. At about the fourth or fifth jig, give the line a quick upward snap. It takes about this long usually for a perch to make up his mind to take your bait, so by yanking automatically you snag him just as he takes it in his mouth. If nothing has the bait, the quick lift helps to attract passing fish and maybe you'll hook one of these with the next snatch. This is strictly a percentage proposition, of course, but it really takes the perch whenever you have them biting reasonably well.

Smelt

Smelt hardly qualify as trophy fish, but they often come in fantastic numbers and this does much to make up for their small size. And crisply fried, they hold their own on a platter with almost any fish you can name.

Small as they are, smelt feed on minnows, though you must have tiny "pinheads" to attract them. These call for constant rebaiting when you have fish under you, so you'll save valuable time if you switch to a tiny slice cut from the first smelt you catch. You don't need a minnow to catch that first one, either; a sliver of salt pork will do as well.

Ordinarily you'll find smelt in deep water—40 feet or more—although they sometimes show up where it's shallower. They are light, fast biters, and you have to keep on your toes to hook them. Use No.-12 hooks and don't try to tend more than two lines. Limber whips like the ones made from bandsaw blade sections help greatly to tip you off to bites. When you have them coming, sit with your hand poised around the line but not touching it. Watch the whip and yank at the slightest twitch.

Here's a little-known tip that will draw smelt to your bait and make them bite faster: Use something bright and flashy for a sinker—a four-inch length cut from the blade of an old table knife, for example. Drill a hole in each end and tie the line in one, the leader in the other. Any scrap of polished or plated metal will do as well, provided it's heavy enough to do duty as a sinker. A shiny object near the bait seems to hold a strange fascination for smelt and draws excited schools to your line. It helps in perch fishing, too. Don't fail to try it!

Until you've caught fish in 40 or 50 feet of water, you won't appreciate how much time you lose in hauling line and letting it out, to say nothing of the work involved. Often you can bring smelt close to the top and this makes your fishing faster and easier.

Let's say that you strike pay dirt at the 50-foot level and the bites come fast and furious. After catching your next smelt, let the line all the way down, then draw it up about three feet and tie a loop to mark the depth. Next time, let the line down to the loop, then bring it up another three feet. Continue to shorten line after each fish as long as you get bites. If you lose the school, go back down and work them up again. In a darkened shanty you can bring them right up to the ice, but they seldom come that close to a hole in the open. Nevertheless, you can generally raise them part way, and each foot means less hauling, faster fishing, and more smelt.

Whitefish

This cousin of the salmon—you can tell him by his adipose fin—doesn't figure greatly in the over-all ice fishing picture, yet he offers winter fun wherever he thrives.

My friends and I fished for perch and pike in a certain lake for years and never caught a whitefish nor heard of anybody else catching one. Then the smelt in the lake multiplied until it made it worth our while to move into deep water after them. There, to our surprise, we began to catch whitefish along with the smelt.

We had fished the deep water for perch, but our baits hadn't been small enough. Not until we used minnows hardly an inch long—sometimes we snipped these in half—and slivers of smelt on No.-12 hooks did we take white-fish. Strange that fish of their size—they average better than a pound—should require the tiny baits used for smelts, but the whole trick of taking them lies in using just a dab.

Whitefish have very tender mouths plus considerable ginger when hooked, a combination which almost always means a lost fish if you merely haul away. We soon learn to yield line when they fought hardest and to draw them in gently after they tired. This enabled us to land most of those we hooked, where before we were losing them left and right.

Whitefish travel in schools and you usually take them in flurries, so watch your lines closely for more bites as soon as the first one comes along. Don't expect heavy tugs; they bite daintily and can skin your hook without your knowing it if you're asleep at the switch.

Decoys

Time, now, to disclose the secret weapon of the shanty fisherman. With windows covered, he sends his decoy zooming into the green depths and lures fish to the top where he can see them and catch them that much easier. His gadget is a rough imitation of a small fish, designed so it planes in wide circles when lowered or raised. With it he lures smelt, perch, walleyes, and whitefish—fish that he would have to go deep for otherwise.

You can't step out and buy a decoy, but you can make one easily enough. From a piece of white pine make a torpedo-shaped body about four inches long and three-fourths of an inch through at the thickest point. Drill a one-eighth-inch hole (or a little larger) from the nose to about two thirds of the way to the tail. Fill the hole with lead so the decoy will sink. Coat with white paint, preferably of the luminous variety, and, if you think eyes are needed, use glass-headed pins or black paint. Cut the fins (see drawings) from a tin can or use other light sheet metal. Grind one end of each fin to a knife edge and drive it into the body. Turn a small screw-eye into the top just ahead of the balance point and snap your swivel to this. You needn't be fussy about the precise shape of your decoy, but you may need to add more lead, change the angle of the fins, or move the screw-eye slightly to make it plane in the widest possible circles. A few experiments will soon put you on the right track.

To decoy fish you should work in a darkened shanty where you can see far down into the water and no surface light

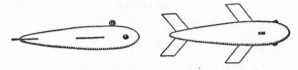

Two views of a homemade decoy

enters the hole to make fish suspicious. Drop your decoy on a loose line to let it sweep as far out under the ice as it will go. Raise and lower the line to make it dart and circle near bottom, then bring it back up in erratic swoops. If you see fish darting about it excitedly, you've tolled yourself a school!

They'll follow all the way to the top. When you have them there, loop your line to a peg or nail so the decoy hangs at the side of the hole just under the ice. This will hold your fish; indeed, the boldest and most excited may dart in to lash at it with their tails! Now, drop your baited hook down to the school and jig it lightly to attract attention. Whenever the fish show signs of drifting off or disappear suddenly, go to work with the decoy again and call them back. Like the girlie-show barker at a county fair, it draws the crowds and readies them for the pitch.

Learn to use a decoy, and you'll not only take more fish but discover a method fascinating beyond compare. You watch your white decoy sink down, down, until you have the illusion of peering from a dizzy height. Then you bring it back, and in the eerie green depths you see flitting shadows—fish, of course, yet no more so than strange, exciting creatures of a different, fantastic world. Fun? You can say that twice!

Fly Fishing

Through the ice? Positively. Definitely.

What's more, you can catch more of some species—bluegills and sunfish in particular—than you can with bait.

The typical ice-fishing fly has a tuft of marabou for a tail and another for wings. A clamped-on split shot just ahead of the tail gives the needed weight, and a wrapping of colored floss makes up the rest of the body. Gantron makes the best body material because of its light-gathering property which results in greater visibility. Use No.-12 hooks if you tie your own, and try various colors.

The tip section of an old trout rod makes an excellent ice-fishing fly rod. Drill a snug-fitting hole in a ten-inch length of broom handle, shove the butt of the tip section in the hole, and your rod is finished complete with grip. Tape an old fly reel to the handle and wind on a ten-yard coil of the lightest nylon you can get—the finer the better, even down to 5X.

Even with this light rig, you won't feel many strikes. Instead, you must "read" the nylon line to know when you have a bite. Let your fly down near bottom, then jig it slowly upward in tiny hitches to imitate the action of a nymph. Continue until you have raised the fly about a foot and a half, then jig it back down again. Due to the natural stiffness of the nylon, your line will coil or spring slightly each time you jig. Watch it carefully; if it suddenly shows more curl, set the hook gently but quickly. For some reason, most fish rise with the fly as they grab it, and strikes show as slight increases in slack. The signal is never pronounced, though, so you must be on the watch to catch it. For this reason some fishermen prefer lines tied from short strands, the knots serving as visible points of reference which make it easier to read bites.

With nylon as fine as 5X you must use care in landing fish. Bring each one into the hole and then flip him out with the toe of your boot while you lift gently with the line.

10. A Few Odds and Ends

Waders

FISHING ALL BUT THE SMALLEST STREAMS IN HIP boots is like rowing with the anchor down, yet a surprising number of fishermen never seem to tumble to this fact. They buy first-class rods, top-quality lines, and smooth-running reels—everything they need for efficient casting—then go only halfway when it comes to the vital matter of wading gear. What a shame!

Watch any hip-booter straining to reach a likely spot. He can keep no more than half a mind on his fishing, for all the time he's dreading the icy flood which momentarily threatens to pour over his boot tops, and he's forever hitching them up to gain another precious inch. No man can fish decently with things like that on his mind.

Chest-high waders free you from that sort of anxiety, but that's not their chief selling point. They let you cover just about double the amount of water, and the extended range is made up largely of those hard-to-reach spots which hold the most fish, to say nothing of the biggest.

For example: You're working upstream with a dry fly and ahead of you lies a long, attractive pool. No fish show in the flat, glassy tail of the pool, but you can see several rising in the faster water farther upstream. Because of the steep, brushy banks, you can't possibly get at them from shore; to lay your fly over those feeding fish you must wade straight upstream. Go as far as a pair of boots will take you and you're still a mile out of range—licked without firing a shot. If, on the other hand, you're wearing a pair of waders, you can approach to within casting distance and probably pick up one or two good fish. Multiply this advantage by the dozens of times you can put it to use in a day's fishing, and you get an idea of the direct bearing a pair of waders has on the size of your catch. Buy chest-high waders by all means; the stocking-foot type and wading brogues if you insist on minimum weight; those with felt soles or hobnails for better traction—but these are beside-the-point considerations at the moment. The big issue: waders, period. Not for looks, not for comfort, but for more fish!

A Portable Boat

A luxury item? No! Once you own a portable craft, it's a cinch that you'll come to look on it as a downright necessity. Since we're out to plug gaps, here's where a boat fits into the picture:

A stream offers 15 miles of trout fishing and gets well flogged throughout its length, save for one particular half-mile stretch. Here it narrows, deepens, and glides through an older jungle—a brushed-choked channel of black water that no fisherman can wade. But talk about trout!

Another stream rises in a swamp—a shaky bog that nobody can penetrate over land. The water, fresh from springs, is clear, cold, and teems with fat native trout.

Then there's the little lake whose mucky, reedy shores have discouraged all building. Drop a bass bug or plug near the lily pads, though, and the largemouths fight to get it. Wonderful bass fishing, but don't come expecting to rent a boat. You bring your own or you don't fish.

That should give you the idea. It boils down to something like this: Probably not more than one fisherman in 100 owns a portable boat, but let's set it at an ultra-conservative one in 25. This means that when you fish water that you can reach only by toting your own boat or canoe—and there's plenty—you're bucking only one twenty-fifth the competition you're up against elsewhere. Take more fish? You can't help it!

For prowling headwaters, bogs, beaver dams, and small ponds for trout, nothing beats the light, maneuverable canoe. The lighter your craft the better, provided it's rugged enough to stand up under normal treatment. After surveying the field, you may decide that an aluminum canoe comes closest to meeting your needs. My own 13-foot Grumman lightweight tips the scales at just under 40 pounds; tossing it on a car or toting it cross-country is a breeze. In six years of hard use it has shrugged off many hard knocks and remains as serviceable as the day it left the factory. Moreover, it has required no upkeep.

If bass fishing's your game, you're best off with a boat—something which will take wind and choppy water better than a canoe, and let you use a motor when necessary. Boats run to slightly heavier weights than canoes, but craft such as the Penn Yan Cartop are light enough for easy transportation, yet give you the stability you need for lake fishing.

A pair of waders and a portable boat or canoe! Once you have your basic tackle, an investment in these two items will bring bigger returns on a fish-per-dollar basis than any other you can possibly make, short of buying a hatchery.

A Fishing Vest

One of the most frustrating experiences in all fishing is to make the sad stream-side discovery that all your leaders (or something equally as vital) are 20 miles away in the pocket of that shirt your wife tossed into the soiled-clothes hamper. This doesn't always happen, of course, but even when you manage to round up all scattered items of equipment, you can't use them efficiently if you have them tucked here and there about your person in makeshift containers.

A good fishing vest quickly solves the problems of mislaid small tackle and sloppy stowage. Once you have one, junk that hodgepodge of enveloped and miscellaneous boxes, then invest in a fly box which will hold *all* the dry flies you carry with you and in a fly book which will do the same for your wet flies and streamers. Your vest will have two large pockets; tuck the dry flies in one and the book of wet flies in the other. Some improvement, isn't it?

A flat plastic leader pouch will hold all the leaders and leader material you'll need for a season's fishing; slide this in beside your fly book. Line grease, dry-fly oil, a bit of ferrule cement, and a spool of winding thread will fit in the smaller pockets, as will eyed hooks, split shot, and any small spinners and wobblers you may wish to carry. Finally, tie a thong to whatever you use to snip leaders and trim flies—a knife with built-in scissors, or one of those gadgets that resemble nail clippers—and loop the thong through a buttonhole before dropping the tool in a pocket.

Whether you fly fish, use bait, rely on the spinning rod, or combine all three, the answer remains the same: settle on a container and place for each needed item, then stick with the system.

Very important: leave everything in place in your vest when you're through fishing. This way you won't have to search the house over for stray equipment the next time you set out, nor will you run the risk of overlooking something essential. Lift your vest from its peg and you have all your small equipment at one grab—a mighty big help when your mind's already on the stream and utterly unfit for anything as exacting as a systematic item-by-item check-out.

Get Out of the Rut

Every trout fisherman has a particular pet stream. He fishes it often, comes to know every pool rip and eddy that is at all likely to hold fish. Or so he thinks.

I, too, have a favorite stream, and for a time it irked me to have others tell of taking trout from this or that spot where I "knew" perfectly well no self-respecting trout would live.

Their claims had the ring of truth, though, so I decided to swallow my pride and do a little investigating. Was I overlooking pay dirt, and if so, how come?

I found the answer my next time out. I started at my usual place, fished the first hole, then worked my way upstream. Just below the next bend I started across the stream.

Working from the "wrong" side of the stream *did* place things in a different light, I found. That dancing current against the opposite bank—the one I usually plowed through—now looked worth a try. I flicked it experimentally with the fly and a good rainbow promptly rose and took it. Astounding!

Thirsting for more of the same, I deliberately avoided my usual route—and took fish where I had never taken them before!

This goes to show that you can never come to appreciate the full potential of a stream until you learn to vary your approach. No matter how you pick your way, you're bound to disturb some worth-while spots in order to reach others. If one fisherman always goes at it one way, and his pal invariably tackles it from another angle, small wonder that they usually fail to agree on where the trout lie.

So, instead of following the same old course along your favorite stream time after time, try others that aren't (to you) quite so obvious. Makes an interesting project and gives you a new slant on things. Has its tangible rewards, too, for every new nook and pocket you discover is another ace you can slip from the pack on those days when trout are especially hard to come by.

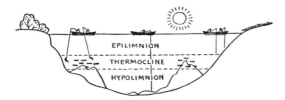

The thermocline

Fishing the Thermocline

In all lakes of moderate-to-great depth you'll find three distinct layers of water during hot weather, each with characteristics of its own. From top to bottom they are: the epilimnion, the thermocline, and the hypolimnion—and for nice, simple names, aren't these beauts? Here's how these three layers come about:

Don't ask me why, but water is heaviest at 39 degrees Fahrenheit. Thus, as soon as the ice goes out in the spring, water at the surface warms until it reaches 39 degrees sinks, and is replaced by colder water which warms and sinks in turn. This mixing process continues until all the water in the lake has reached the 39 degree mark, then no more turnover occurs. Additional warming of the surface water now increases its buoyancy and there gradually develops a floating layer of warm water which deepens as the season advances. This, of course, is the epilimnion. The hypolimnion, or bottom layer, is composed of the cold water which remains sunken due to its greater density. Out of range of the sun and unable to absorb oxygen from the air, it remains uniformly cold and soon becomes stagnant.

Sandwiched between the two is a thinner layer wherein the temperature drops sharply in but comparatively few feet of descent. In other words, this layer—the thermocline—bridges the gap between the warm epilimnion and the cold, stagnant hypolimnion.

All this would matter little if it had no bearing on fishing, but it does indeed. In hot weather, when fish find the top layer too warm for comfort, they head downward, not into the stagnant hypolimnion, but into the thermocline where they find comfortable temperatures, sufficient oxygen, and food. This can well mean that at certain times of the year you fish in the thermocline—whether by design or accident—or you take no fish!

This important layer can lie at various depths, depending on the size of the lake, the time of year, and other factors, so there's no sure way of locating it without the help of a maximum-minimum thermometer, an inexpensive little instrument which records the highest and lowest temperatures with which it comes in contact. Here's how you work it:

Maybe the surface temperature is 78 degrees; lower the thermometer ten feet and haul it back up. It reads 76 degrees. Since this is not a significant drop, lower it another ten feet. This time it registers 72 degrees. Drop it five feet and it reports 62 degrees. Another five feet—52 degrees. Whoops! The thermocline! You should find fish between the 20- and 30-foot levels. Bear in mind that this is a hypothetical example; the thermocline may lie deeper, or even nearer the surface. No matter, fish it wherever you find it.

Don't expect to take fish by dropping down into the thermocline any old place, though. Fish find much of their food on or near bottom, so the most likely fishing spots will be where the bottom lies within the thermocline. For example, the thermocline in our imaginary lake rested between the 20- and 30-foot levels. There your best chances would come by fishing in water 20 to 30 feet deep, not by fishing with 25 feet of line with the bottom 60 feet beneath your boat.

A depth chart—try your state fish and game department—is a great help in identifying the best areas. By noting where the depth falls within the thermocline range you can choose a likely site for still-fishing, or plot a course for trolling which will keep your lure in promising water practically all of the time.

It would be foolish, of course, to say that all fish hang to the thermocline 100 percent of the time. Lake Trout may go far below it whenever the bottom layer holds sufficient oxygen. Trout and landlocked salmon may gather at spring holes or at the mouths of cold streams, while largemouths and the pikes tolerate warm surface water long after it has driven down cold-water fish. Nevertheless, an increasing number of fish of nearly all species seek relief in the thermocline as the top layer steadily grows warmer and the bottom layer loses its oxygen, or, if they don't do so for comfort, they drop down to feed on the bait fish which congregate there. So, when the surface fishing falls off in July and August, go to work with your thermometer. Find the thermocline, and you'll find the fish!

The Best Time to Fish?

Best, of course, would be to fish *all* the time, but few are that lucky. The rest of us must grab each chance as it comes along, then make the most of it. Never, while a spark of life remains, do we intentionally let precious fishing time go to waste, but we sometimes do it unwittingly. Let's look at trout fishing for a moment.

Everybody's in a fit and a fever to hit the streams on Opening Day, and this high enthusiasm continues through the peak of the season. The big hatches come during that first month or month and a half, the fish are rambunctious, but the competition is terrific. With warmer weather, the water levels drop, hatches become fewer and fewer and the fishing slackens . . . *but so does the fishing pressure!* For the fellow who can cut the mustard with a fly rod, the two effects just about cancel each other; the trout may not feed as ravenously as they did when the big hatches were on, but there's no longer an army of fishermen to keep them nervous and jittery.

A few streams, of course, become so warm that fishing is next to hopeless, but most give you the chance for some of the most interesting fishing of the season. Work slowly and carefully—you'll have the water to yourself—with small flies, delicate leaders, and long casts, and you'll find that tag-end-of-the-season trout fishing can be every bit as rewarding as the earlier variety.

For a one-shot test, try closing next season with a bang, just as you open it. Get out while the roosters are tuning up for the day, and fish as hard as you do on Opening Day. Bet you wind up with more trout!

The same goes for bass and pike fishing, only here you have the added incentive of stepped-up feeding on the part of these fish when the water cools in the fall. Surprisingly few fishermen take advantage of this; for the majority, fishing ends on Labor Day and that's that. The fishing picks up and the competition folds—what better chance could you ask!

Now that we've skirted all around the question, let's face up to it: When *is* the best time to fish? On the average, but not invariably, you'll get your best fishing at dawn and at dusk. Fish tend to greet the first light of a new day with a lapse of caution born of hunger, and they again grow bolder when the deep shadows of twilight have given them a feeling of increased security.

This, alas, doesn't mean that you're a sure winner if you rise early, stay late, or both. Fish have days when they feed eagerly, others when nothing seems to tempt them, and those when they show a moderate interest in food.

The various fishing charts seek to name these days in advance: the best, the poorest, and those which are only so-so. More specific and to the point are the Solunar Tables which hedge not at all, but point to the precise hours of each day when (according to them) fishing will be the hottest. Though daringly presumptuous, such charts and tables hit things on the nose just often enough to satisfy the thousands who swear by them, yet manage to look silly with sufficient regularity to delight their equally numerous critics. Thus, as additions to fishing lore, they could hardly have more charming characteristics.

If this leaves the question of when to fish unanswered, it is probably better so. The angler finds sport in fishing only because its mysteries have remained mysteries, and its gods merry, capricious, and whimsical. Give him his rod and water to test his skill; he'll ask no greater boon than his fair share of Fisherman's Luck.